T0177188

DO IT
ANYWAY
DEVOTIONAL

DO IT ANYWAY DEVOTIONAL

60 Days to a Bolder Faith

Tasha Cobbs Leonard

with Travis Thrasher

WATERBROOK

CONTENTS

CONTENTS

DO IT
ANYWAY
DEVOTIONAL

DISCOVER IT

Her sister, Mary, sat at the Lord's feet, listening to
what he taught.

—LUKE 10:39

My father, Bishop Fritz Cobbs, was a man of very few words. He was an eloquent and moving speaker when he gave messages behind the pulpit and a constant encourager to the members of his church. But I knew that since Dad was a man of action rather than words, it was that much more important to take in the lessons he taught me. One, which I'd heard from childhood, was, "Baby, stay at the feet of Jesus."

This counsel comes from the story of Mary and Martha in Luke 10. Jesus had arrived in Bethany, and Martha invited Him and His twelve disciples into her home. As the one managing this household, Martha wanted everything to be perfect. Jesus wasn't just any ordinary houseguest; He was the Son of God! So she did what she thought she needed to do: worked hard to host a special meal for their guests.

However, Martha's younger sister, Mary, chose to do something different. She sat before Jesus to listen to His teachings. This upset Martha, so she went to Jesus and said, "Lord, doesn't it seem unfair to you that my sister just sits here while I do all the work? Tell her to come and help me" (verse 40).

I can picture Jesus smiling at Martha when He replied, "My dear Martha, you are worried and upset over all these details! There is only one thing worth being concerned about. Mary has discovered it, and it will not be taken away from her" (verses 41–42).

I believe that so many times we open the door and invite Jesus in to be a part of our lives, but when He shows up, we don't take the opportunity to sit at His feet. Instead, we feel as though we have to keep working and moving and acting. *I know my purpose and I gotta move toward it,* we tell ourselves. But then we act without hearing from God and knowing what He wants from us.

I know that before I move toward my purpose, I need to sit before Jesus to hear from Him. This is why my father gave me this instruction repeatedly over the years. He knew it was the best advice he could give me.

We need to focus on coming before Christ to hear what He wants us to know. We need to kneel at His feet and worship Him. We need to fix our eyes upon Him first and foremost, and then worry about everything else afterward.

Have you discovered the importance of sitting at Jesus's feet? Do you find it easy to come before Him, or do you keep your hands and your mind so busy that you forget to do this?

This devotional is all about this very simple illustration of sitting at the feet of Jesus. What does this look like daily? It's not just about listening for His Word. It's about worshipping Him. It's about honoring Him. It's about praying to and pleading with Him. It's about boldly and confidently living out the instructions and wisdom He gives us.

PRAY

Heavenly Father, thank You for letting me come before You to listen and to learn. Forgive me for the times I'm too busy to focus on You. In Your name, amen.

2

PURSUE IT

One day as Jesus was walking along the shore of the Sea of Galilee, he saw two brothers—Simon, also called Peter, and Andrew—throwing a net into the water, for they fished for a living. Jesus called out to them, "Come, follow me, and I will show you how to fish for people!" And they left their nets at once and followed him.

—MATTHEW 4:18–20

"Follow me."

I can visualize Peter and Andrew on the shoreline, standing with their dirty nets and their sweaty brows. I imagine them watching Jesus as He walks up to them and tells them to follow Him so they can learn "how to fish for people."

It seems as if they instantly dropped those nets and did what Jesus asked. Was it that simple and easy?

For the disciples and others to whom Jesus spoke, it seems that making the decision to follow Him was easy. As Jesus said in Luke 9:23, "If any of you wants to be my follower, you must give up your own way, take up your cross daily, and follow me." Such a simple decision to make. Of course, Peter and Andrew demonstrated that following Jesus comes at a price. Their lives testify that "the gateway to life is very narrow and the road is difficult" (Matthew 7:14).

Jesus doesn't say that following Him will be easy, but He still asks us to do it.

My song "I Will Follow" speaks to this sort of faith. I can imagine those disciples saying to Jesus the very same words: "I'll follow where You lead. Your hand I trust completely. You can lead me. Where You lead I'll go."[1]

Can you say that?

If Jesus walked up to you today, could you easily drop whatever nets you're holding?

Could you suddenly, without any fear or reservation, say that you will follow your Lord and Savior?

"I'll follow where You lead."

Along with the rest of the disciples, Peter and Andrew trusted Jesus wholeheartedly. For three years, Jesus took His disciples on an amazing journey. They saw miracles, watched wonders, learned truths, and witnessed the glory of Jesus. They saw Him nailed to the cross. And then they saw Him risen.

To come to the feet of Jesus, we first must follow Him. We must trust in and obey Him.

Pursuing Jesus wholeheartedly is a decision we make today and again tomorrow and every day after. And we know that someday we will see Jesus in His full glory, seated at God's right hand.

PRAY

Dear heavenly Savior, thank You for the gift of Your Son, Jesus. Thank You for allowing me to follow Him. Help me follow You with all that I am, and grant me Your mercy when I fail to follow You. Help me be bold and pursue Your feet, Lord. In Jesus's name, amen.

3

READ IT

Righteousness guards the person of integrity,
but wickedness overthrows the sinner.

—PROVERBS 13:6, NIV

Many things in life come with instructions, but how many of us actually read those manuals? We buy a new dishwasher, plug it in, and start pressing buttons. We get that new flat-screen television, grab the remote, power it on, and never look back. Or we purchase a new vehicle, leaving the five-hundred-page manual unread in the glove compartment for months—until one of those little warning lights pops up on the dashboard.

A few years ago, one study revealed that only 25 percent of people read the manuals for the products they buy. Not only that, but the study also found that consumers don't use all the features on these products.[1]

My pastor likes to refer to the Bible as a manual from God that guides us through our lives. It's our how-to book on living life well—living righteously. The problem is that many of us don't focus on righteousness in our walk with Christ.

I realize that the word *righteousness* may sound high and mighty—something unattainable, something we can't touch. But Scripture is our manual for righteousness. Righteous living is evidence of a God-loyal life. I love how *The Message* describes this in Proverbs 13:6: "A God-loyal life keeps you on track; sin dumps the wicked in the ditch."

We may be heading in the right direction, but something suddenly distracts us. It leads us off the right path and may try to put us in a ditch—or in a dark place that's difficult to get out of. A God-loyal life keeps us on track.

I want to encourage you that the Word of God is where you'll find exactly what you need. The Bible is our instruction manual to live righteous lives so that we won't find ourselves in that dark, sunken place where it's hard to recover.

PRAY

Dear sovereign Lord, thank You for providing me with a manual that shows me all I need to live a godly life. Help me use your Holy Word as a daily guide. In Jesus's name, amen.

4

KNOW IT

*In his grace, God has given us different gifts for doing
certain things well. So if God has given you the ability to
prophesy, speak out with as much faith as God has given
you. If your gift is serving others, serve them well. If you
are a teacher, teach well. If your gift is to encourage
others, be encouraging. If it is giving, give generously. If
God has given you leadership ability, take the
responsibility seriously. And if you have a gift for
showing kindness to others, do it gladly.*

—ROMANS 12:6–8

"How do you define yourself?"

If someone asked you this, what would you say? Would
you define yourself by your job? Perhaps you're a teacher
or a pastor or an artist. Maybe you would say you're a par-
ent or a student. But deep inside, *Who are you really?*

I've always seen myself as a worship leader. In fact, this
is why I *didn't* want to sign a record deal at first. Even after
making my first independent album, *Smile,* I had no aspira-
tions or desire to sign with a record label. I felt like it might

taint the purity of my worship. God, however, wasn't so concerned.

A gospel artist named Myron Butler was working on an album, and he'd been watching videos of various up-and-coming artists on YouTube. He saw a video of me leading worship and reached out to ask if I would be interested in being a part of his album being recorded live in Dallas. I agreed and hopped on a plane. When the time came for me to sing my part in "Not My Own," I mounted the stage and began to belt out the lyrics. Something special happened during that live recording. God showed up in a mighty way. For fifteen minutes as we worshipped, people were on the floor, crying and lifting their hands. Each time that happens, I walk off the stage praising God for always showing up!

In the audience, among those worshipping, were people from Myron's label. They greeted me with enthusiasm and told me that someone had sent them my first album. They hadn't listened to it but were planning to. I left that day not expecting anything would come of it, but just a few days later, the president of the label called me.

"We have your album, but there's nothing that can compare to what we experienced in person," he told me. "I want to put you on every stage we can—on every platform we can—to do exactly what you did that night."

Then he asked me a question that changed my view of signing a record deal: "How do you define yourself? Are you a worship leader, or are you an artist?"

I smiled. "I'm a worship leader."

"Then we will sign you as a worship leader."

This man didn't know me or my heart. However, I'm sure he could sense that I was afraid of signing a deal, so he assured me he didn't want me to change anything. I knew who I was, and my assignment was to lead worship!

He kept his promise not only about how I was defined but also about giving me the opportunity to do what I was purposed to do around the world. That was how God broke down the walls for *Grace* to be released. That record deal made it possible for me to share songs like "Break Every Chain" with people everywhere. I didn't have to change who God made me to be.

So let me ask you again: How do you define yourself?

The first step in answering the question is knowing what God wants from us. As it says in Romans 12, God has given each of us different gifts. What gifts and talents has He given you? Are you using them well?

Learn to recognize what God has planned for your life. Celebrate your gifts and talents. Never let anybody—the critics or the cynics or the chatterboxes of this world—make you doubt your identity. Don't let anyone else define you. You are shaped and defined by our Master Creator.

PRAY

Dear heavenly Father, thank You for making me exactly how You wanted me to be. Help me be confident in who I really am in You. And let me always be able to serve You well with my gifts. Amen.

5

ACCEPT IT

Wait for the LORD;
be strong and take heart
and wait for the LORD.

—PSALM 27:14, NIV

Perhaps you've seen the 1984 classic movie *The Karate Kid*. A martial arts master named Mr. Miyagi promises to teach karate to a high school student named Daniel who's being bullied. For the initial lesson, Miyagi surprises Daniel with his request.

"First, wash all the cars," Miyagi says. "Then wax. Wax on—"

"Why do I have to—" Daniel starts to protest.

"Ah ah! Remember deal! No questions!"

Miyagi instructs Daniel, "Wax on . . . wax off."

It always frustrated me to see the martial arts master make Daniel do these menial tasks that seemingly had nothing to do with karate. But they proved to be surprisingly valuable instructions.

Daniel's story in *The Karate Kid* reminds me of David's story in 1 Samuel. Though David was anointed king as a young man, it's estimated that he had to wait another ten to fifteen years before actually becoming the king.[1] In the meantime, he returned to the fields where he looked after sheep. Surely, he had moments when he felt like he was doing something that a king shouldn't be doing. But this was significant to his purpose!

If David had never fought off a lion or a bear, he may never have had the confidence in God to defeat a giant. For the people to realize there was something special about this boy, David had to tend the sheep before he could step into the palace.

Sometimes we're like Daniel and David, frustrated about where we're at in life and wondering about our purpose. Perhaps you think you don't *have* a purpose because you're in a season that seems to have nothing to do with what you feel like you've been called to do.

I've been in that season before. Midway through college I decided to return home to Jesup, Georgia, where I ended up becoming a manager at a video warehouse store for two years. I felt a calling on my life for leading worship, and many times I wondered why God had me working at a place where people came to rent movies. I couldn't have imagined that I *needed* this season of management so that I would one day be able to pastor a church with my husband.

My job—my identity—at that video warehouse didn't seem to line up with what I was called to do. But it was all on purpose for *my* purpose!

There are seasons in our lives that feel confusing and even frustrating. Seasons where we ask God, *What are You trying to teach me? This doesn't feel like what You promised me.* But we can trust that God has a very good reason.

PRAY

Dear Holy God, help me be content in the season I'm in right now. Reveal what You want in my life, and help me know that You are always in control of everything, big and small. In Jesus's name, amen.

6

HIDE IT

I have hidden your word in my heart,
that I might not sin against you.

—PSALM 119:11

It's never been easier to hear from God.

You can grab your phone, open a Bible app (if you don't have one, I encourage you to download one!), and read any verse in seconds. You can google any passage of Scripture and reference dozens of translations. There are videos that have celebrities reading Scripture, audiobooks of the entire Bible, and television shows you can stream that dramatize God's story. And, of course, there are the printed Bibles in our homes and churches and libraries.

The living Word is more accessible today than ever before.

But at the same time, we live in a busy world full of distractions and dangers brought about by technology. The Enemy is only a tap away, waiting to deceive and disturb and ultimately defeat us. That's why we need to rely on the Word of God even more each day. That's why we need to hide Scripture in our hearts.

Consider what your typical day looks like. Most of us find it hard to regularly designate time to be still and present before God, to meditate on Scripture for even a few moments.

I've discovered that I love to listen to the Bible while I'm getting ready in the morning. I pick my favorite app where I can listen to someone reading from any passage I choose. This practice is beneficial in my busy life to maintain my spiritual growth. I'm often surprised that even when I hear the same scriptures over and over again, I can still get a fresh revelation from God. That's why the Bible is called the living Word. It speaks to us *today*. It speaks to us in the moment.

Amid all the busyness, how can you make time for God's Word? Does it mean taking a break from social media to instead scroll through Scripture? Perhaps follow someone who encourages others with Bible passages. Maybe do what I do and listen to the Bible while getting ready for work. Find something that works for you. Be vigilant about it. Hide Scripture in your heart—repeat it to yourself, memorize it, sing it, write it on note cards. Listen to the same passage every day for a week to meditate on it.

Growing up, I didn't need a Bible app—I had my father. The Word of God was embedded in his heart. He was a Bible teacher and emphasized how important it was to hide the Word of God in my own heart. That's my foundation. And that's what I pass to you: Make Scripture your foundation.

PRAY

Dear heavenly Father, thank You for giving us your Holy Word. Help me find ways to hear from You daily, so that I can guard my heart and protect my mind. In Your Son's name, amen.

7

CARRY IT

Dear brothers and sisters, be patient as you wait for the Lord's return. Consider the farmers who patiently wait for the rains in the fall and in the spring. They eagerly look for the valuable harvest to ripen. You, too, must be patient. Take courage, for the coming of the Lord is near.

JAMES 5:7–8

Hopes and dreams are like songs. Sometimes they arrive quickly, appearing out of nowhere and surprising us. Sometimes they develop slowly over time. Sometimes we almost forget about them. But God knows the desires of our heart. The Lord is always good to those whose hope is in Him.

When I was seventeen years old, our entire family went to visit my aunt in Columbus, Georgia, who was battling breast cancer. One morning my mother came running down the stairs, tears streaming down her cheeks. "God gave me this song," she told us.

Then she began to sing: "In one place, in one tabernacle, with Jesus. There is no other place where I'd rather be than in one place, in one tabernacle, with Him."

We were all astonished. It was the first song she had ever written. We were in tears listening to her sing and worshipping the Lord with her.

"I don't know if it's finished," Mom said. "But I think this will make a beautiful song."

She was right. The inspiring lyrics and the moving melody were amazing. They were an incredible start to a song. Yet for so many years, the song remained unfinished and unheard.

For my first album, *Smile*, I tried with everything in me to write verses to go with that song. But it never worked. The same thing happened with the next album, *Grace*. For years I carried that song inside of me, wondering if it would ever see the light of day. For seven years, I lived with that partial song. But I never gave up on it.

In October 2014, ten months after losing my father, I began recording my next album. I told the producer about the song my mother had written when I was a teenager, a song I'd been trying to complete for a long time.

"Just go back and try again," he told me.

Not long after that, I was asleep one night when— *boom*—I woke up with a melody: "I'm here because I wanna be."

Oh my God—that's it!

It took so many years to get the verses to that song, "One Place."[1] But I never gave up on it.

We all carry things like that in our lives. Ideas. Goals. Desires. Things that seem to take *forever*. Hopes that sometimes never seem to be fulfilled.

Still, we must trust God's timing. We must put our trust in Him for *everything* and continue to hope and dream. As Galatians 6:9 says, "So let's not allow ourselves to get fatigued doing good. At the right time we will harvest a good crop if we don't give up, or quit" (MSG).

The seed of hope will one day be harvested! Keep carrying that song, that dream, in your heart. Never let go of that chorus, because one day the verses are going to come!

PRAY

Dear heavenly Father, help me find peace in You. Help me find joy in Your presence. Help me pursue Your will. Help me always want to be where You are, so I can give You every hope I have. In Jesus's name, amen.

8

USE IT

In a well-furnished kitchen there are not only crystal
goblets and silver platters, but waste cans and compost
buckets—some containers used to serve fine meals, others
to take out the garbage. Become the kind of container God
can use to present any and every kind of gift to his guests
for their blessing.

—2 TIMOTHY 2:20–21, MSG

We all carry an assortment of tools inside of us that are
waiting to be used. For me, I know that God uses music as
one of His tools to reach the world. Over the years, people
have told me after services that, even though a message
might have spoken to them, the song I sang ministered to
them in the way they needed. Music is a powerful tool.

Throughout the Bible, God often used different tools
for His glory. He used the staff that Moses carried. The
trumpet blown by Gideon. The sling David used to kill Goliath. Imagine all the tools used by King Solomon's crew to
build the temple. And then there were the beams, bolts,
bars, and doors used as Nehemiah oversaw the rebuilding
of Jerusalem's wall.

Nowadays it seems like there is a tool, gadget, or gizmo to fix or do anything. Building and repairs have never been easier! But there is a whole other universe of tools we may not have considered: social media. Social media can be a vessel, like our Bible verse says, but we must remember that "some containers [are] used to serve fine meals, others to take out the garbage."

We have to be careful with social media and keep it in its proper place. We must not allow it to become a god or define who we are. Although it can be used as a tool for the kingdom of God, it can also become a weapon for the Enemy.

When my label encouraged me to get on TikTok, I thought they were crazy.

"I'm too old for TikTok," I told them. "I'm already maxed out on Instagram."

I didn't want to be on camera all the time and put on makeup every day just to do some videos. I had a kid to raise! I saw the platform as one more responsibility I didn't need to add to my plate. But God had other plans (like He often does!). After much persuasion, I decided to create an account, and then I put out a TikTok of me. However, the video wasn't of me singing; it was a clip of me teaching at our church. I thought, *Maybe I can share some of God's hope with a few people today.* So I sent my words out to the world.

God's about to make your dreams so real, that your doubters will be speechless. Don't stop dreamin' because others don't believe. If you gotta believe alone, keep dreamin'. Somebody say, keep dreamin'. If I'm the only one who believes in it, everybody else laughs about it, I'm gonna keep dreaming.[1]

It felt like I blinked and the video had one million views. I couldn't believe it.

It can't be that simple!

But anything is simple for God. Social media is just like song melodies—both can be used for God's glory.

Do you have the gift of humor? It's a tool. Are you good in the kitchen? How about the ability to teach children? Or a special way with numbers? Or an incredible eye for creating visual art? All of those are tools.

What tools has God given you in your toolbox? How can you use those today for His glory?

PRAY

Dear God, thank You for all the gifts You give us. Help us celebrate those gifts and see how we can use them to share Your love with others. In Jesus's name, amen.

9

SEE IT

We know how much God loves us, and we have put our trust in his love.

   God is love, and all who live in love live in God, and God lives in them.

—I JOHN 4:16

When was the last time you used a filter on one of your photos? Be honest. I'm not talking about the kind that turns you into somebody else but the one that smooths over the wrinkles and softens the skin. The kind that gives you that perfect glow, that radiant grin.

Don't we sometimes treat our lives this way? Setting the filter to perfection so that the world sees us in the best light possible? I can relate because I did this for many years.

I was a pastor's daughter. I believed I had to put on a mask of perfection. I needed to get straight A's in school. I had to look my best and present myself well. I could never make a mistake. I needed to be a good example to others. I needed to be good . . . *at everything!*

Those were heavy weights of responsibility for a ten-year-old kid! I grew into adulthood thinking that I wasn't allowed to be flawed, believing that I had to be perfect to meet others' expectations. But here's what I found out: Perfection is impossible. When you try to be perfect—putting on so many masks—you later end up at a place where you don't even know yourself. You wake up one day and think, *Who am I?*

I eventually reached a point in my life that many others so often arrive at: a place of brokenness and isolation. I knew I was gifted, but emotionally I was crushed. For years I had bottled up the deep-rooted feelings I had been denying—feelings of rejection and unworthiness—and suddenly I didn't know where to find Tasha in the midst of all the clutter. I thought nobody cared. I believed that only my voice and my songs were what people wanted from me and all I had to offer.

I realized I needed to get rid of those rotten filters and find out who Tasha really was. So I did what my daddy told me to do: I put all those emotions and wounds at the feet of Jesus.

When we lay our flaws and incapabilities at His feet, that's where we find strength. That's when we see ourselves as God sees us. We are His masterpiece, His wonderful handiwork! When I finally looked through God's filter, I discovered the true Tasha—and I actually liked who I found!

What sort of filters do you put on your life? Do you carry different filters for different people and places? How does God see you right now? Can you show that person off to the rest of the world today?

PRAY

Dear gracious Lord, thank You for creating in me a masterpiece that brings You glory. Help me be happy with myself, and give me the strength today to be a light to others. In Jesus's name, amen.

NAME IT

This is what the LORD says—
  he who created you, Jacob,
  he who formed you, Israel:
"Do not fear, for I have redeemed you;
  I have summoned you by name; you are mine."

—ISAIAH 43:1, NIV

We know the names of God from the Scriptures. He is called *Jehovah*, which means "I Am Who I Am"; *El Shaddai*, which is "God Almighty"; *Adonai*, meaning "Master" or "Lord"; and *Immanuel*, which means "God with us." Each of God's many names gives us a picture of who He is.

And the amazing thing is, God knows *your* name! This mind-blowing truth inspired my song "You Know My Name," co-written with my dear friend Brenton Brown. When we worship, we are responding to the goodness of God. We are confessing His name because of how much He means to us. And we mean something to Him—more than we could possibly fathom!

I wrote this song as a reminder. A reminder for me and a reminder for you. Sometimes we need reminders. Sometimes life can be stressful and our faith can be stretched and even strained. Other times life can become an emotional wildfire, when our faith becomes engulfed in the thick smoke of fear and failure.

No matter who you are and no matter what is happening, God *knows* you.

If you're sitting with a heavy heart, God *sees* you.

If you're praying for that friend in need, God *hears* you.

If you're looking at your checkbook wondering how you're going to pay your bills, God *stands* beside you.

If you're weary and worn down, God *holds* you.

If you're afraid for tomorrow, God *comforts* you today.

We might know the names of God, but do we truly trust what they mean?

If He truly knows Tasha, then do I truly know Jehovah Shalom, "the Lord is Peace"?

If He truly sees Tasha, then do I truly see Abba, my heavenly Father?

Let's do what Hagar did in Genesis 16 when she called out to the Lord by the name "El Roi" and proclaimed, "You are the God who sees me" (verse 13).

God sees you right now and knows your name. Never forget this.

PRAY

Dear God—Immanuel—thank You for being with me. Thank You for knowing me and watching over me and loving me despite how I disregard You and run away. Help me remember that You long for us to call You by all Your names. In Jesus's name, amen.

11

SAY IT

This is the day that the LORD has made.
We will rejoice and be glad in it.

—PSALM 118:24

Can you hear the song in your head, the hymn you might have sung as a child, as you read today's verse? "This is the day, this is the day, that the Lord has made, that the Lord has made . . ."

It's such a beautifully simple psalm, yet it is a positively powerful declaration. In our world full of negativity and divisiveness, we need to make it a habit to speak uplifting and optimistic words out loud.

My family is mindful of our speech and our language. Starting at the beginning of each week, we speak positivity into our days. "This is going to be a great week."

We believe it too.

"We're going to accomplish everything we set out to accomplish this week."

Can you say that as well? Go ahead—say it out loud.

What you'll find is that the things you speak start to happen. But that's not because of your own strength and power.

It's not because of your strong mindset. It's because you know that this day and this week have been created by God.

Speak or sing Psalm 118:1: "Give thanks to the LORD, for he is good! His faithful love endures forever."

Do you see God's goodness in your life and in the lives of your loved ones? Do you find that His faithfulness never ceases to amaze you?

Do you believe that the Lord is *for* you? That He will help you through anything?

When you lean on the reality that the Lord is your strength and your song, He will give you the victory! Psalm 118:25 says, "Please, LORD, please save us. Please, LORD, please give us success."

When you declare that this is the Lord's day and you ask for His mercy and blessing, then you can believe that He will give you success according to His will and grace.

So rejoice today! Rejoice and be glad in it!

PRAY

Gracious heavenly Father, thank You for today. Thank You for all You have given me and all You're doing in my life. This is the day You have given me; I rejoice and am glad in it. Let me declare the hope I have in You and share this with others. In Your Son's name, amen.

12

BELIEVE IT

Humanly speaking, it is impossible. But with God everything is possible.

—MATTHEW 19:26

Some days it's difficult to come before the Lord trusting that He's fully and completely in control. Sometimes it's a struggle to see God's light shining through the dark clouds hanging over us. Some days it's hard to believe.

Have you ever been there? Are you there right now?

I understand. I've been there before. And there's something I've learned about being human: We put expectations on God, often without realizing it. We tend to set a timetable around His promises and His blessings. But sometimes those promises and blessings don't turn out the way we expected. Sometimes God tells us, "I want to do it *this* way."

There's nothing too heavy or too difficult for the power of God to break through. But we often try to break through barriers ourselves, forgetting that we're not on our own. We neglect to remember that Christ alone can do all things.

After Kenny and I went through the long and arduous process of trying to start a family, only to see it fail, all we could do was trust that God had a plan. We prayed and believed. When we decided to begin the adoption process, once again all we could do was pray and believe.

Things eventually worked out in a glorious way! They didn't happen the way we first expected them to happen, but God came through with His own amazing plan. It reminded us that even when our greatest hopes don't come true, God is still working and His ways are still good.

This is where my song "Gotta Believe" was birthed. It's a declaration of faith. Say it over yourself today:

> *I just gotta believe*
> *There is goodness around the corner*
> *And something better is in store for me*
> *Someday I will see*
> *There's a reason for all these tears*
> *And there's an answer to these prayers.*[1]

Believe it and boldly declare it. Believe that one day you will be stronger. Believe that there is going to be more to your story. Believe that God will work things out for His glory.

In the midst of darkness and pain, you can believe with confidence that God is going to work things out better than you could ever have imagined!

PRAY

Loving God, thank You for being in control. Thank You for being faithful to Your promises despite how much I might doubt that You are. Please give me the patience and the persistence to keep believing in You. In Jesus's name, amen.

13

WEAR IT

As God's chosen people, holy and dearly loved, clothe
yourselves with compassion, kindness, humility,
gentleness and patience.

—COLOSSIANS 3:12, NIV

I'm a self-proclaimed fashionista. What I'm wearing reflects the relationship or space I'm in. I can get all dressed up for a Sunday morning service or decked out for a red carpet awards show, and then the next moment kick off the high heels and kick it in some new sneakers. On the days when I'm home with my kids, I'm in comfy sweatpants or a muumuu.

Clothing is mentioned frequently throughout Scripture. One of the opening chapters in the Bible speaks of God being our very first fashion designer: "The LORD God made garments of skin for Adam and his wife and clothed them" (Genesis 3:21, NIV). But most of the time, the reference to outer garments is used as a metaphor or an illustration.

> Put on the full armor of God, so that you can take your stand against the devil's schemes. (Ephesians 6:11, NIV)

Anyone who has two shirts should share with the one who has none, and anyone who has food should do the same. (Luke 3:11, NIV)

Do not consider his appearance or his height, for I have rejected him. The LORD does not look at the things people look at. People look at the outward appearance, but the LORD looks at the heart. (1 Samuel 16:7, NIV)

Our faith is the fabric that should cover us daily. Because we represent Christ, what we wear should represent Him well. He is our defense and the epitome of generosity, compassion, kindness, humility, gentleness, and patience.

People see *you* before they can see God in you. So here is my encouragement: In the morning, as you're putting on your outfit for the day, remember to also clothe yourself in the attributes that represent Christ.

PRAY

Dear loving God, thank You for giving us illustrations that demonstrate how we are supposed to live as believers. Help me represent You today in my appearance, my actions, and my attitudes. In Jesus's name, amen.

14

QUESTION IT

GOD, are you avoiding me?
Where are you when I need you?
—PSALM 10:1, MSG

Do you ever wake up feeling the weight of this world? Perhaps before your eyes even open, you can see the endless assortment of difficulties and doubts that await you. You have a never-ending, unrelenting To-Do List of Trouble that never seems to go away. Deep down, do you find yourself questioning where God and His comfort and guidance are? You're in good company. All throughout Scripture, God's people asked Him questions. The book of Psalms is full of them:

> O Lord, how long will you forget me? Forever?
> How long will you look the other way?
> How long must I struggle with anguish in my soul,
> with sorrow in my heart every day? (13:1–2)

David wasn't struck down dead for bearing his heart and searching for God's answers to his struggles. But just a few verses later, David declared,

I trust in your unfailing love.
I will rejoice because you have rescued me.
I will sing to the LORD
  because he is good to me. (13:5–6)

That's the tough part: worshipping even though we are weary and praising even when a part of us wants to panic.

We all go through heavy seasons. Dark times. Certain experiences that have us questioning our faith. We may not understand the heaviness right now, and we may question God. But that's okay! I don't think God is afraid of our questions. We can ask good and deep questions. And I believe every single day, God reveals His wisdom to those looking for it. He might not reveal all of it, and we might not be able to comprehend everything, but He is patient with us as we come to Him to watch and listen.

The disciples waited in darkness and fear after watching their Lord and Savior be crucified and die on a cross. After Jesus's resurrection, He came back and appeared to the disciples. When they freaked out, thinking they were seeing a ghost, Jesus calmed them.

" 'Why are you frightened?' he asked. 'Why are your hearts filled with doubt?' " (Luke 24:38). He told them to look at His hands and His feet to know that it was really Him, to literally touch Him to make sure they knew He was real. Then Jesus said something remarkable: "Do you have anything here to eat?" (verse 41).

No grand entrance, no bright lights and smoke machines and theme music. Jesus walked in and said, "Guys, it's really Me! Calm down. I'm hungry. Let's sit and eat and talk together."

So today, tomorrow, and the rest of your life, feel free to ask God questions. Feel free to wonder where He is and what He is doing. Then invite Him to speak to you. Linger in His presence and listen for the things He needs to tell you today. There are times when we need to wait on God, just like the disciples had to wait when Jesus said, "Stay here . . . until the Holy Spirit comes and fills you with power from heaven" (Luke 24:49). But those times are never wasted. If you wait and trust in Him, God will give you the strength to overcome any doubts you have in your life.

PRAY

Savior God, please hear my prayers and my questions and my requests. And, Lord, please speak to me today. Open my heart and help me hear what You have to say. Thank You for being in control of every aspect of my life. In Jesus's name, amen.

15

DO IT

Whatever you do, work at it with all your heart, as working for the Lord, not for human masters.

—COLOSSIANS 3:23, NIV

One of the most famous slogans is Nike's "Just Do It." I've always loved it, especially since one of my slogans is "Do It Anyway."

The first woman to ever sign an endorsement deal with Nike's Jordan Brand was Maya Moore. She was a high school hoops legend in Gwinnett County around Atlanta, Georgia, who went on to greatness at the University of Connecticut and later the Minnesota Lynx. While playing for the UConn Huskies, Maya chose 23 for her jersey number.[1] This was Michael Jordan's number, as well as LeBron James's number, but that's not the main reason she chose it.

During Maya's senior year of high school, she noticed one of her All-American basketball friends signing autographs with Colossians 3:23 underneath. She loved this and decided that it would be her life verse. "No matter what I was doing," Maya said, "no matter who was or wasn't watching, I'd give my best with my whole heart because I knew it pleases the Lord, who gives me my breath and gifts. I thought this could be a meaningful message that I could share with people every time I signed something for them."[2]

Not everybody has a platform where the whole world watches. People may not be asking for your autograph today, but don't be fooled; more people are watching you than you realize. Your friends, colleagues, classmates, kids, siblings, parents, neighbors—they see the way you live your life. So consider this: What is your life slogan? What is the message, theme song, or verse you want your life to proclaim? How can you show that to the rest of the world?

PRAY

Oh, God, fill me with Your Holy Spirit. Let my life be a testament to Your power and goodness. Give me the words to speak to others. Inspire my actions and my interactions with others. Thank You for all You do. In Jesus's name, amen.

16

TRY IT

Whenever we have the opportunity, we should do good to everyone—especially to those in the family of faith.

—GALATIANS 6:10

I still remember the moment. All these eyes looking at me, waiting for my answer. All these faces staring with expectations. All my friends wondering what I was going to do.

"Tasha, you gotta sing," someone said again.

"What are y'all talking about?" I asked, shaking my head. "I'll *direct* it. But I am not leading this song."

I was fifteen years old and a member of a community choir. We were at a church ready to worship when we learned that our lead singer had been involved in a car accident. I couldn't believe they were asking me to stand in front of everyone and lead a song! But I reluctantly took the microphone, closed my eyes, and started to sing.

Imagine if I had continued to say no. Imagine if I had made someone else take that microphone. Who knows how my life would have unfolded?

Our lives are full of moments like this. Times when we have an opportunity to do something that feels a bit terrifying. It might not be singing in front of a crowd. It could be anything—taking a new job, going on a first date, or even applying for a job. We all have moments when we can take a chance—a chance where we might perform well or fail miserably. Too often, our fears prevent us from taking that chance. Other times it's our pride. Or perhaps our stubbornness to change. Or our lack of faith.

God gives us moments where we are able to find ourselves. Times in our lives where possibility shows up. The question is whether we will embrace that possibility.

When I finally opened my eyes after singing and saw the response from others, I knew something had changed dramatically in my life. People were worshipping and weeping and praising God. I couldn't believe what I was seeing. But God had seen it all along.

God sees you and knows you. There will be times when you're asked to step up, to stand out, and to do something new. What will you do with those opportunities? Don't think of it as just an opportunity to build your confidence. This may be God moving you into your calling.

Whatever opportunities you encounter, remember that it's not about having faith in yourself as much as it's about having faith that God is going to make great things happen.

Watch for those opportunities—big and small. One simple yes can change your life forever.

PRAY

Loving God, thank You for the opportunities You bring my way. Help me know Your will and courageously embrace new experiences. I ask in Your Son's name, amen.

17

CREATE IT

O LORD, what a variety of things you have made!
In wisdom you have made them all.
The earth is full of your creatures.

—PSALM 104:24

What is your passion? Do you enjoy teaching or preaching? Maybe you're a singer or a storyteller. Perhaps you love technology or fixing things. Or maybe you are always making culinary delights in the kitchen.

I encourage you to take your passion and create something out of it.

Maybe you would welcome this challenge. But some of you might be thinking, *How am I going to do that? I don't have the time or the resources to create something!*

Years ago, two friends presented me with this same challenge. I was twenty-five years old and living in Atlanta when they invited me to lunch. I had barely even looked at the menu when they began talking about my passion.

"When are you going to do this album?" they asked.

There were many topics I assumed we would chat about, but my making an album was definitely *not* on that list. Sure,

I had been writing and singing a lot of songs while leading worship with other churches, but this subject caught me off guard.

I don't know the first thing about recording an album!

I had never thought about channeling my passion into an album before that moment. But once the idea was introduced . . . it would *not* let me go! That night, feeling the strong pull and creative energy, I wrote out a plan for recording a live album.

Did I know what I was doing? Nope.

Did I do it anyway? Absolutely!

That strong pull was the Holy Spirit moving through my friends and transferring on to me. And that invitation and spark of creativity gave birth to my first album.

Now let me stop you if seeds of doubt are already spreading into your creative soil. Don't think of the obstacles and all the reasons why you shouldn't create something.

Instead, know that God put that passion in your heart for a reason. Consider how you can be a blessing with that passion. What can you create to bring goodness, truth, beauty, or change to the world?

The idea isn't to create something that will draw attention to ourselves. No. It's to do what God has done by creating us. As Psalm 104:24 says in *The Message,*

> What a wildly wonderful world, GOD!
> > You made it all, with Wisdom at your side,
> > made earth overflow with your wonderful
> > > creations.

We are His wonderful creations. So let's go out and celebrate that by creating something wonderful for Him!

PRAY

Dear Creator God, we praise You for forming the sea and the sky and all the creatures of the world. Inspire me to make something that brings You glory and encourages and challenges those around me. In Jesus's name, amen.

OWN IT

Don't be afraid. I know you're looking for Jesus the
Nazarene, the One they nailed on the cross. He's been
raised up; he's here no longer. You can see for yourselves
that the place is empty. Now—on your way. Tell his
disciples and Peter that he is going on ahead of you to
Galilee. You'll see him there, exactly as he said.

—MARK 16:6–7, MSG

My original degree when I went to college was in early childhood education. Lord help me! Now, I was on point with the teacher part; I was born to be a teacher. But *early childhood* education? There is just not enough patience in the world to give me a career teaching little boys and girls!

Maybe I'm not called to open a daycare, and maybe you're not called to be an astronaut. But when it comes to fulfilling our calling by faith, we should *never* feel like we are underqualified. In case you need some reminders, let's just open the Bible and skim through the books.

There was Abraham. He was way too old to be the "father of many nations."

And look at Joseph. His brothers tossed him away like the morning's trash. How could God use him in any way?

Moses was a murderer with a speech impediment living in the wilderness. And he was supposed to lead the Israelites out of Egypt?

Rahab? Others wouldn't have expected God to use a prostitute.

Nehemiah? How could someone who served as the king's cupbearer be qualified to rebuild the city walls of Jerusalem?

And Peter. Oh, Peter. So headstrong at times, but then suddenly heading in the wrong direction after denying Jesus three times. How could he be used mightily for the Lord?

One of my favorite "underqualified" women from the Bible is Mary Magdalene. She was the woman Jesus delivered from seven demons. Surely she wasn't ever going to be used by God. But not only did Mary serve Jesus in His ministry; she was the one who delivered the news to the disciples that He had risen from the dead! Think about that opportunity, that assignment!

God doesn't look at our résumés or check out our social media accounts. He doesn't make a list of our strengths and weaknesses. Instead, He looks at our hearts. He knows none of us are qualified to spend eternity with Him. That is why He offers us grace. That's why He gave us His Son. He asks us to use what we have, the opportunities, gifts, and experiences He's given us, to do the work He's placed in our hands.

Never fear that God can't use you. Never hesitate to be the person telling others that the One nailed on the cross has been raised from the dead!

PRAY

Savior God, thank You for choosing us to proclaim the good news. Thank You that I don't have to be qualified to be chosen, and that You are working through me in more ways than I can see. In Jesus's name, amen.

19

RECEIVE IT

Because of his great love for us, God, who is rich in
mercy, made us alive with Christ even when we were dead
in transgressions—it is by grace you have been saved.

—EPHESIANS 2:4–5, NIV

Grace is an unexpected gift left at your doorstep on a depressing, frustrating day. The note reads, "I love you and I adore you and I'm watching over you—God."

Grace is a call after a catastrophic day with a voice on the other end gently telling you, "I've got you, and I'm going to sustain you."

Grace is something we get that we don't deserve. It's something we can't work for or beg for. Grace is something that only God gives, and it's because of His mercy and love.

"Daily grace saves me," as the song says. "But for Your grace, I would be lost if it wasn't for Your grace."[1]

Wherever you are today, remember that God has covered your life with grace that gives you the strength to do what you're called to do on this earth. Grace is available to us daily, but we must choose to *receive it daily*.

Grace doesn't tell us we're great. It reminds us of the opposite. We can't do anything—*anything*—without His power. We would be lost . . . but for His grace.

I'm honored to be called to lead people into the awareness of God's presence. Every day I'm grateful that God continues to overwhelm me with the grace to do so. I am humbled that He would even choose me with all my imperfections.

God doesn't have to offer us grace. But He chooses to give us grace every day. His unmerited favor keeps coming—every day.

PRAY

Faithful Father, thank You for the gift of grace. Thank You for loving me, for sending Your Son to die for me, and for giving me the gift of eternal life with You. Thank You for Your never-ending grace. In Jesus's name, amen.

20

FIND IT

Oh, the joys of those who do not
follow the advice of the wicked,
or stand around with sinners,
or join in with mockers.
But they delight in the law of the LORD,
meditating on it day and night.
They are like trees planted along the riverbank,
bearing fruit each season.
Their leaves never wither,
and they prosper in all they do.

—PSALM 1:1–3

Joy. Don't we all long for it? On our good days, we bask in it; on our tough days, we might get only fleeting glimpses of it. Deep down, our souls yearn for joy, yet we can't experience it on our own.

Psalms—a book of prayers and praises often quoted by Jesus and the apostles—begins with the secret to finding joy. Many translations of Psalm 1 begin with "Blessed is the one . . ." or "Blessed is the man . . . ," but I love how the

New Living Translation starts off Psalms: "Oh, the joys of those . . ."

For all the songs and poems of lament and frustration, the Psalms are ultimately a book about finding the joy, the blessing, and the happiness that God wants for us. To do that, we are first instructed what *not* to do: Don't be guided by the godless, don't imitate sinners, and don't echo scorners.

Instead, we are to delight in God's Word and think about it day and night. Or as my dad said, "Baby, stay at the feet of Jesus." It was the greatest lesson my father taught me.

When we sit at the feet of Jesus and settle our spirits, we hear instructions on how to live our lives and how to move forward. This practice resembles those thick trees planted along the riverbank, spreading out and growing. They aren't just a picture of prosperity; they are a portrait of peace.

This is what God wants for us. Peace. Joy. Blessings.

He watches over us and wants the best for us. "The LORD watches over the path of the godly, but the path of the wicked leads to destruction" (Psalm 1:6).

Find the path that leads to the feet of Jesus. Walk that path daily to the place where you find joy and blessing.

PRAY

Dear Father, thank You for the joy of spending time with You in Your Holy Word. Thank You for the delights You give me. Forgive me when I forget to sit at Your feet. In Jesus's name, amen.

21

HEAR IT

*Pay close attention to what you hear. The closer you
listen, the more understanding you will be given—and
you will receive even more.*

—MARK 4:24

When was the last time you heard God speaking to you?
Did His message confirm something on your heart, or did
His Spirit surprise you with His command?

I was twenty-three years old when God surprised me.
Shocked me, in fact. I had left college to come back home to
Jesup to help my dad with his church. Our youth ministry
was growing like crazy. I was learning and growing, and I
knew this was where I needed to be. This was what I was
called to do. Then I attended a leadership conference in Atlanta with my parents and heard a very clear message from
God: *You have four months to move to Atlanta.*

*Why, God? That makes no sense. What's in Atlanta? I'm
comfortable here.*

Everything in Jesup was familiar. The path in front of
me seemed clear. When I thought about the move to At-

lanta, however, I felt like I was stepping into a hazy fog. But I realized *that's* exactly when we have to trust God.

Even when you can't trust what you see, you have to know what you've heard. I moved to Atlanta on a word from God, but first I had to be open to hearing and trusting His voice.

Is the noise in your life preventing you from trusting what you've heard from God? Does the busyness of your day distract you from God's presence?

To live a bold faith, we need to remember Jesus's charge to His followers and pay close attention to what He has spoken to us. And then we need to follow Him.

PRAY

Heavenly Father, thank You for speaking to us in good times and bad times. Please help me hear You today and trust what You've already spoken to me. In Jesus's name, amen.

22

WANT IT

Since you have been raised to new life with Christ, set
your sights on the realities of heaven, where Christ sits in
the place of honor at God's right hand. Think about the
things of heaven, not the things of earth.

—COLOSSIANS 3:1–2

"What do you want today?"

If someone asked you this, what would you say? I imagine your answer would vary based on who was asking. For instance, if your mom asked, you might request that she come over and watch the kids, or you might invite her out to lunch. If your spouse asked you, you might suggest a date night, a back rub, or breakfast in bed. If your boss asked, you might petition for a promotion or support on a challenging project.

But what if Jesus knocked on your door and asked you the same question? What would you tell your Lord and Savior who is able to look into your heart and mind and knows everything that weighs on you?

If Jesus asked you what you want today, would your response be aligned with His will? Would you ask for that promotion or dream house, or would you ask for guidance about how to help someone else? Would your request be to gain more followers on social media or more wisdom from Him?

Deep down, do your desires rest in this world? Do you desire to spend more time with the Father, or is your schedule already filled? Do you find comfort in your favorite sports team or music group? Or are you seeking refuge in God?

God already knows the desires in our hearts. I challenge you to set aside space in your day for an honest moment with God. Ask Him to give you an eternal perspective to inform, shift, or grow your desires. Focus more on His greatness than on all the "great" things this world offers us. As it says in Colossians 3:11, it doesn't matter who you are—rich or poor, famous or unknown, a king or a prisoner—because "Christ is all that matters, and he lives in all of us."

PRAY

Almighty God, please shape my desires and dreams to align with Your will rather than the world's. Forgive me for pursuing foolish things instead of pursuing You, and direct my focus to the fullness and goodness of Your kingdom. In Your Son's name, amen.

23

BEHOLD IT

Look, God is greater than we can understand.
His years cannot be counted.
He draws up the water vapor
and then distills it into rain.
The rain pours down from the clouds,
and everyone benefits.
Who can understand the spreading of the clouds
and the thunder that rolls forth from heaven?
See how he spreads the lightning around him
and how it lights up the depths of the sea.

—JOB 36:26–30

Every day provides an opportunity for us to see God's wonders. We must simply look up. Each day the sky is filled with a different canvas. Feathery and faint, fluffy ripples, white cotton, gray gloom—clouds are a confirmation of the glory of our almighty Creator.

Clouds are gatherings of water droplets suspended in the sky. We can have science explain them, but let's be real—it's a marvel that thousands of pounds of water tower above us every day. Sometimes the clouds pour that water, but for the most part, they float and span the horizon.

The most spectacular viewing times for clouds are sunrise and sunset. That's when the sun intensifies their color and shape. They suddenly become a vibrant yellow or a glowing orange or a brilliant red. That's when it seems like God is really showing off. Like He's telling us, *See what I can do? I can do this all day long. I'll do it tomorrow, and I'll do it the next day, and each time will be different and delightful!*

Job 36:26 says, "Take a long, hard look. See how great he is—infinite, greater than anything you could ever imagine or figure out!" (MSG).

Too often, we forget to take long, hard looks. We even forget to take peeks. We keep our eyes locked on our little worries and neglect to look up in wonder. Scripture tells us, "Lift up your heads, you gates; be lifted up, you ancient doors, that the King of glory may come in" (Psalm 24:7, NIV).

Today, take some time to behold God's beauty in the masterpiece mounted in the heavens and remember the majesty of the Lord.

PRAY

Dear Lord God, I praise You for Your splendor and Your magnificence! I exalt Your power and Your glory. Thank You for all You have created. Thank You for creating a masterpiece in me. In Jesus's name, amen.

24

RECOGNIZE IT

We know that in all things God works for the good of those who love him, who have been called according to his purpose.

—ROMANS 8:28, NIV

Today's verse is one of the most well-known and beloved verses in the Bible. But as familiar as this verse is, as I was reading it one day, God revealed something new to me.

I reread it many times and focused on the words "in all things God works for the good." I had always thought that if something was happening to me, its original intent was for my good. But God showed me something different.

I took the things that were intended to hurt you, the things that were intended to bring you pain, and I worked them for your good.

It was like God was the middleman standing in the gap. And I began to think of some of the experiences from my life and from others' lives—moments of pain and agony and suffering. The hurts and the letdowns and the traumas. In all those situations, God didn't use those moments to revel in our pain; rather, He used them to reveal something to us.

This is your opportunity for Me to do something new in you.

This is your opportunity for Me to show you a miracle that you've been waiting for.

Consider the story of David and King Saul. There were so many times when Saul hurt David—so many times he tried to kill David—but God didn't tell David to focus on what the king was doing to him. Even when David had a chance to kill his enemy, he said, "Don't kill him. For who can remain innocent after attacking the LORD's anointed one?"[1] Those were seasons of preparation for David to be the king that he was called to be. It wasn't about what someone was doing *to* him. It was about what God was doing *in* him.

The hurtful, disappointing things that have happened to you, that are happening to you today—God is working through them for your good.

So in those moments when we're hurting, the question we should be asking is this: *God, what do You want me to learn in this situation?*

Yes, there is hurt and brokenness, but God is using it and working it for your good.

PRAY

Faithful God, thank You for working in my life even when I don't see it. Help me recognize that You work everything for Your glory and my good. I praise You for loving me enough to be working in my life. In Your Son's name, amen.

25

DISPLAY IT

*To Him who is able to do exceedingly abundantly above
all that we ask or think, according to the power that works
in us, to Him be glory in the church by Christ Jesus.*

—EPHESIANS 3:20–21, NKJV

"Tot, get up."

For a moment, I felt like I was having an out-of-body experience. I was hovering over myself and my cousin Shanicka at the Grammy Awards in the Staples Center, and I had just heard a name I recognized.

That sounds like my name, but this can't be happening.

Finally, after hearing Shanicka and feeling her nudge, I stood and accepted my Grammy for Best Gospel/Contemporary Christian Music Performance. The whole situation was surreal and unimaginable, especially since my father had passed away just five days earlier. I had never expected to be in the limelight, and after hearing the news of my father's death, I didn't *want* to be in the public eye. Yet I was there because I knew my dad would have wanted me to be there.

I was functioning on his encouragement for me to *Go and do it anyway.*

My father had always been an example of moving forward in your life regardless of what obstacles and difficulties you may be facing. I know God's timing is perfect, so in the midst of my grief, I chose to get up and keep going. It's often easy to preach about God's peace and about the power of God that works in us, but it's another thing to walk that out in our lives. Especially when the world is watching.

This is why we must remain at the feet of Jesus. During the high moments and the low moments. The noisy seasons and the silent seasons. Even when things are difficult and we don't think we can get up, Christ will give us the strength to do so. He will give us that nudge to keep going. With God, we are stronger than we realize.

When God gives us a chance to represent Him, we need to take that chance. And when we put Him on display, He never fails us.

How has God done exceedingly abundant things in your life? How can you boldly trust this in your life today?

PRAY

Faithful God, thank You for delivering me through my darkest, toughest moments. I praise You for Your power and Your protection over me. Today, help me come to the feet of Jesus and give You the glory. In Your Son's name, amen.

26

EXPRESS IT

*Encourage each other and build each other up, just as you
are already doing.*

—I THESSALONIANS 5:11

Take a second and consider how fierce your pace of life is
these days. Perhaps it's breezy and sunny, or maybe it's a
little faster but still manageable. Or are you spinning out of
control at the catastrophic speed of a Category 5 hurricane?

When my father passed away in 2014, I was in a season
in which I was operating on a Category 5 level in terms of
just how engulfed I was in my work. I've joked that I was
probably sitting at the Grammys sending out emails. I was
never present. Never. Life was exploding around me in a
good way, yet I never slowed down. But my father's death
forced me to do just that.

After our family began therapy during our grieving
process, I remember the therapist telling me, "I want you to
tell your family and loved ones what you're going through."

She gave me an exercise to walk all of them through, a
way for them to make *me* be present. During whatever moments I might be experiencing in my life, whether they were

dark or amazing, my family and friends were to ask me how I was feeling. It might be related to something monumental or it might be something minor. Since I have some issues with my toes, my husband sometimes asks me, "Are your toes hurting?" It helps me to be there in the moment.

"Are you excited?"

"Do you feel nervous in your stomach?"

"Do you have too much on your plate?"

"Hey—where are you?"

My loved ones now ask me all sorts of questions to make sure I'm present with them. And I made a commitment to give honest answers. I became adamant and intentional about allowing those around me to *help* me.

I'm much more present now, especially with my family. I don't want to live that Category 5 life. I don't want to be the mom who looks back and thinks, *Oh my God, I missed five years of my kid's life.*

What about you? How present do you feel with the people God has placed around you? Do you find it easy or difficult to connect with your loved ones? What might it look like to invite your close friends and family to check in with you, and to check in with them, to help one another stay present during those busy winds of life?

PRAY

Holy God, thank You for my life and for all those You have brought into my world. Help me be present with them, and let them help me during the season of life I am walking through. In Your Son's name, amen.

27

PRAY IT

Pray without ceasing.

—I THESSALONIANS 5:17, NKJV

Never stop praying. That's what the apostle Paul instructed in his letter to the Thessalonians. Three simple words, right?

But what does that look like? Do we need to get on our knees and spend an hour crying out to our Lord and Savior? Maybe.

But it's more than that. We also need to speak to God in the morning, during the day, and at midnight (if you're awake like I am). Prayer should not be designated to some allotted time as if it were an activity like working out or picking up coffee. It's not a to-do item that we simply check off our list. We should be in a constant conversation with our Creator.

I encourage you to thank God at the start of the day for all He has given you. Ask Him to watch over you and your loved ones. Pray that God will give you the daily strength to live up to your potential.

Throughout the day, allow your heavenly Father into your head and into your heart. Let His Spirit check you when you need to be checked. Let Him take control when your spirit wants to take charge. Let God know that you *need* Him!

When you make a mistake—and Lord knows we're *all* going to make mistakes—confess it to the Lord. Ask for forgiveness in Jesus's name. Be honest. Be real. Be repentant.

Bring God your hurts. Tell Him about your pain. Ask for monumental miracles. As Jesus said in Matthew 7:8, "For everyone who asks, receives." God listens and He answers. We might not know how and when, but Jesus makes it clear that anyone who prays for something will receive an answer.

Perhaps you're thinking of the times you have prayed but God never replied? Does your praying seem to be met with only silence? Let me remind you what Bishop T. D. Jakes wrote: "God remembers you. I know you may find that difficult to believe, but hear me: He remembers you. He has always remembered you!"[1]

The problem isn't that God doesn't remember us. It's that too often we forget about Him. We're too busy with our own lives, with the news and the noise of the world, with our interests and our instant gratifications. We forget the Friend and the Father we have watching over us.

So today, don't forget to do what that beloved hymn says: "What a privilege to carry everything to God in prayer!"[2]

PRAY

Gracious God, thank You for the gift of prayer. Thank You for listening to me, and for answering me in Your way. Help me remember to pour out my heart and my mind to You daily. All day long. Without ceasing. In Jesus's name, amen.

28

IMAGINE IT

After this I saw a vast crowd, too great to count, from
every nation and tribe and people and language, standing
in front of the throne and before the Lamb. They were
clothed in white robes and held palm branches in their
hands. And they were shouting with a great roar,

> *"Salvation comes from our God who sits on the throne*
> *and from the Lamb!"*

—REVELATION 7:9–10

Imagine being able to get a sneak peek of what heaven looks like. Take a moment to picture this scene from Revelation where multitudes stand celebrating our almighty God. Can you hear the majestic sound of all those voices united in worship? The very sight would take our breath away.

My father had a saying when he preached. Anytime he spoke about heaven, he would say, "If I ever get a glimpse, I'm not coming back." It wasn't that he wanted to leave his family and his church behind. Rather, he was expressing the beauty of wanting to be with Christ. That was his heart.

He knew what Psalm 84:10 states: "A day in Your courts is better than a thousand. I would rather be a doorkeeper in the house of my God than dwell in the tents of wickedness" (NKJV).

My father passed away unexpectedly on January 19, 2014. Since then, my mom and I have talked a lot about what my dad used to say about heaven. We think that he did indeed get a glimpse. He saw the incredible joy that awaited him in glory, so he made that choice, knowing that one day he will see us when we get there.

This isn't just a comforting thought to help us in our grief. We still miss him every day. But we know that he is worshipping right now in heaven, declaring what it says in Revelation 15:3–4:

> Great and marvelous are your works,
> O Lord God, the Almighty.
> Just and true are your ways,
> O King of the nations.
> Who will not fear you, Lord,
> and glorify your name?
> For you alone are holy.
> All nations will come and worship before you,
> for your righteous deeds have been revealed.

Pause for a minute and picture what awaits you in glory. What are you most looking forward to? What do you imagine it will be like to walk and create and sing in the light of God's holy throne?

PRAY

Dear gracious God, thank You for giving me an idea of what awaits me in heaven. Let my focus be on eternal things and not on temporary things on this earth. In Your Son's name, amen.

29

RELEASE IT

Come to me, all of you who are weary and carry heavy
burdens, and I will give you rest.

—MATTHEW 11:28

What loads are you carrying today? Maybe it's a burden of loss. Maybe you're overwhelmed with work and responsibilities. Maybe it's simply all those heavy loads of laundry you have to do. Whatever you're hauling today, remember this: God will help you do the heavy lifting.

Sometimes I picture our burdens as icebergs in the sea of our lives. We're moving along steadily and then spot something that seems minor. But 90 percent of an iceberg is unseen, hidden beneath the water. Not knowing the size, we strike it and get hurt. We become broken. And sometimes we're broken for a long time.

We try to do it on our own—but this never gets us far, does it?

In my song "Burdens Down," I sing about how we try to carry our hurts and our bad habits with us, how we get to a point of becoming sick and tired of all our pain.

This is when we finally hear Jesus telling us, "Come to Me . . ."

This is when we need to lay our burdens down, to trade our shame in for a crown.[1]

Imagine taking the load you're carrying and bringing it before the cross. Picture it being lifted off your shoulders before the glory of Christ.

As believers in Christ, we are not meant to carry any load alone. But Lord knows we try. We get busy and lost and messed up and miserable, and suddenly we're climbing up a mountain with a five-hundred-pound sack on our back.

Lay your burdens down. Bring them before the Lord. Find rest in your relationship with Jesus. This is His promise. This is His desire.

PRAY

Dear Savior, I praise You for the gift of peace. Please help me place my burdens before You, however big or small they might be. Let me know the comfort You give to all those who come to You. In Jesus's name, amen.

30

SHOW IT

*Imitate God, therefore, in everything you do, because you
are his dear children. Live a life filled with love,
following the example of Christ. He loved us and offered
himself as a sacrifice for us, a pleasing aroma to God.*

—EPHESIANS 5:1–2

When I first signed with a record label and recorded *Grace*,
a woman who worked with the label told me something I'll
never forget: "You're different."

I didn't understand what she meant, so she explained it
to me.

"I have worked with so many artists, and their ministry
has never really impacted me. Not until now."

When I heard this, it broke my heart. I thought, *Wow,
these people distribute gospel music. They produce it and they
listen to it all day, every day. And here she is, telling me that it
hasn't impacted her!*

I decided that day that the life I lived in front of her
would be the same life I lived on stage. I was all for it! It
wasn't that I wanted others to believe that I'm some sort of

super-Christian. I wanted the people who distributed this music, managed store counters, and worked backstage to also encounter God. I still want that now.

Each of us has a calling—not just in one arena but in all arenas. When we are at work, we need to be the same people we are in our homes. The person who goes to that concert should be the same one who shows up in church the next morning. Whether we are intentional about it or not, we are showing others what it looks like to be Christians.

Everybody—every single person—needs Jesus. We each have a calling, and we can never forget that every day we encounter human souls looking for hope. We might not even think our interactions have all that much importance to influence them in any way, but God might be thinking differently. God has put them in your life for a purpose. Never forget this!

PRAY

Dear Lord God, I praise You for being in control of everything. Please help me see opportunities to be a witness for You and a blessing to others wherever I am. Today, give me the strength to boldly share my faith. I ask in Jesus's name, amen.

31

SING IT

You know that God paid a ransom to save you from the empty life you inherited from your ancestors. And it was not paid with mere gold or silver, which lose their value. It was the precious blood of Christ, the sinless, spotless Lamb of God.

—1 PETER 1:18–19

Redemption. It's a glorious thing. When we fully see and understand God's love for us, our eyes open to His infinite mercy.

Fanny Crosby saw this even though she was blind her whole life. As she said in her autobiography,

When about six weeks old I was taken sick and my eyes grew very weak and those who had charge of me poulticed my eyes. Their lack of knowledge and skill destroyed my sight forever. As I grew older they told me I should never see the faces of my friends, the flowers of the field, the blue of the skies, or the golden beauty of the stars.[1]

Crosby's disability never broke her delight in her Savior. At the young age of eight, she wrote this about her condition:

> Oh, what a happy soul am I!
> Although I cannot see,
> I am resolved that in this world
> Contented I will be.
> How many blessings I enjoy
> That other people don't.
> To weep and sigh because I'm blind
> I cannot, and I won't.[2]

Fanny Crosby is one of the most well known and beloved hymnwriters, who wrote more than nine thousand hymns. These include songs like "Blessed Assurance" and "To God Be the Glory." She lived from 1820 to 1915, and perhaps the only thing more amazing than all the hymns she wrote was the joy she poured into them.[3] The pure joy that comes only from redemption.

In her hymn, "Redeemed," she wrote of being so happy in Jesus and thinking of Him all day long: "I sing, for I cannot be silent; His love is the theme of my song."[4]

Oh, to be filled with the same joy this woman of God had! To wake up seeing the beauty of God despite hardships and disappointment. To delight in God's presence and to know He is guiding our steps. To praise God for giving us songs in the dark of night!

PRAY

Gracious and good Father, thank You for redeeming me. Thank You for sending Your Son to die for my sins. I praise You for the gift of praise and worship. Help me sing Your praises all day long. In Jesus's name, amen.

32

FIGHT IT

The LORD is my shepherd; I shall not want.

It's easy to fall into the trap of entitlement our culture has encouraged.

Perhaps someone has told you, "You *deserved* that blessing!"

Or you've thought to yourself, *I've worked hard and I earned that!*

Our expectation of what we deserve is one of the major tensions we fight in this world. We see entitlement everywhere, even in the church. We are often as spoiled as we can be! And with social media influencers and instant everything, it can be easy to fall prey to the feeling that we deserve more.

Oh, I deserve this. I went to school for this. I worked hard for this. It's my time!

Too often, we hear the "me, me, me" of discontentment in our heads. But what if God were to give us what we *really* deserve? Oh, Lord! Thank You, God, for Your mercies every day!

We must remember that God is the prize and everything else is an added blessing.

We should always come to Him in humility and reverence.

Instead of approaching the promises and privileges we are given as if they belong to us, we should begin each day with a heart of contentment and gratitude. Instead of focusing on ourselves—on what we can do and what we can get—we should daily remember Lamentations 3:22–23: "The faithful love of the LORD never ends! His mercies never cease. Great is his faithfulness; his mercies begin afresh each morning."

The way to fight entitlement is by keeping a posture of humility. The kind of humility that causes us to come to the feet of Jesus knowing that everything we have is because of Him. We don't deserve anything, and God knows that. And yet He gives us so much. He gave us His only Son. He gives us eternal life with Him. He's given us all that we have and more.

PRAY

Holy God, thank You for Your gift of grace. Forgive me for feeling entitled and for taking credit for all the things You've done in my life. Help me always come before You in humility and reverence. In Jesus's name, amen.

33

SHARE IT

In You, O LORD, I put my trust;
Let me never be ashamed;
Deliver me in Your righteousness.

—PSALM 31:1, NKJV

Pause for a minute and be honest with yourself. How are you doing right now?

When people ask how we are doing, the cultural default is to simply say, "Fine." But so many of us are *not* fine. We carry our pain and our problems hidden deep inside. It's easy to hide behind social media posts, nice things, and busy schedules. But so many of us feel like we are losing a constant war, and we beat ourselves down so much that we never feel like getting back up. Shame can do that to you.

I know because I've been there.

It's easy to show people the glitz and the glamour, but for many years I struggled with depression. For days, I would be home in bed, with fear and anxiety keeping me in the dark. But here is something I've learned . . .

Empathy is the killer of shame.

Shame *bows* to empathy.

I discovered this from Dr. Brené Brown's book *Dare to Lead,* where she said, "Empathy is the most powerful and connecting and trust-building tool that we have, and it's the antidote to shame. . . . Empathy creates a hostile environment for shame—an environment it can't survive in."[1]

Shame messes with your mind, telling you that you're the only one dealing with this. That this is too much for you, that you can't handle it. But the moment you hear someone tell you that they've struggled with the same thing—that's when you experience freedom. When someone empathizes with you, it helps you see the light at the end of the tunnel. That's how I made it back to a healthy space mentally.

But the only way to experience empathy is to be transparent. Being honest about our struggles and challenges allows us to receive love from others. We can't receive hope and encouragement if we don't open ourselves up to it.

I've been very transparent about my battle with depression and weight issues to encourage others. I want people to know that they are not alone, and that there's hope. Here's the truth: *We all are battling with something.* Maybe it's just a thorn in your side. Maybe it's something that you must overcome daily. Maybe it's a minute-by-minute choice. But you're not alone.

You never know how many people might be blessed when you are open and transparent with what's going on in your life. When we are transparent, we have an impact on people's lives because they know they're not alone. And they will see that God can heal anybody going through anything.

PRAY

Dear almighty Savior, thank You for seeing my pain and my problems, and thank You for healing me again and again. Let my transparency today create pathways to receive and give encouragement. In Jesus's name, amen.

34

EMBRACE IT

*You are a chosen people, a royal priesthood, a holy
nation, God's special possession, that you may declare
the praises of him who called you out of darkness into his
wonderful light.*

—1 PETER 2:9, NIV

If God chose only the purely righteous to occupy heaven,
the kingdom of heaven would be an empty place. As Romans 3:10 states, "No one is righteous—not even one." But
praise God that anybody can enter those pearly gates, even
those who spent much of their life raising hell! Nothing dis-
plays God's grace like the sudden transformation of an un-
godly soul.

Thomas Ryman was the wealthy owner of a riverboat
company and a prominent Tennessee businessman. By 1885,
he had a fleet of thirty-five steamers, all stocked with liquor.
He benefited from the city of Nashville being overcrowded
and full of gambling, prostitution, and crime. So when a revival took place on a May night in the city and drew thousands of locals, Ryman went to see what the commotion was
all about.[1]

Sam Jones, a traveling evangelist, was speaking that night, and his message changed Ryman's life forever. The businessman left the revival meeting with a new purpose in life: to make sure Nashville had a proper place where people could gather and worship God. He vowed to build a church large enough to hold every person who wanted to hear Reverend Jones.

Ryman's mission resulted in the Union Gospel Tabernacle, completed seven years later in 1892. As Reverend Jones stood behind the pulpit for the first time to preach, he said, "This tabernacle is the best investment the city of Nashville ever made."[2] After Ryman passed away in 1904, the building was named after him. This is how Ryman Auditorium was created.

When I first went to the Ryman, I didn't know its amazing history. I just knew we were making history! It was such a privilege to be the first ever to record a gospel album in that theater. When I learned that the beautiful brick church was originally built as a revival center, I knew it was the perfect match for the theme of the album we were making. That album is called *Royalty*.

When God gave me the title of *Royalty*, I didn't realize just how meaningful and relevant that theme would be. Scripture reminds people of who they really are: holy daughters and sons of God who can rise and be resurrected from any season.

No matter who we are or what we've done, God never changes the way He looks at us. He sees His children as royal. He paid the cost so we can be royalty, so we can spend eternity with Him in glory. This royalty has already been given to us; it's up to us to embrace it.

That message changed the life of Thomas Ryman. He spent the rest of his life trying to honor the Lord. Are you in a season of life in which you don't feel worthy of God's love? What's holding you back from receiving God's unconditional love for you? When you choose to believe and trust that you truly belong to the Lord, your faith will grow. You will feel like royalty. And God will give you a mighty mission in life. Just watch for it and embrace it!

PRAY

Dear gracious God, thank You for saving me from my sins. I praise Your name! Help me make the choice today to fully embrace Your love for me. May I step into the purpose You have for my life. In Jesus's name, amen.

35

GIVE IT

*After this interview the wise men went their way. And the
star they had seen in the east guided them to Bethlehem.
It went ahead of them and stopped over the place where
the child was. When they saw the star, they were filled
with joy! They entered the house and saw the child with
his mother, Mary, and they bowed down and worshiped
him. Then they opened their treasure chests and gave him
gifts of gold, frankincense, and myrrh.*

—MATTHEW 2:9–11

When I was about fifteen years old, my father began a tradition of having a "Happy Birthday, Jesus" celebration at our
church. On Christmas night, people would come to worship. Like the wise men who came from the east, each person would bring gifts that God had blessed them with to
give back to Him as an act of worship. It was a beautiful
experience every year.

Christmastime can be a joyous occasion to reconnect
with family and friends and to celebrate Jesus's birth. Giving gifts to one another is an act of love that honors Him.

When it's done in the right way, I believe Jesus is delighted. Unfortunately, the Christmas holiday can also turn into a stressful and chaotic season and be celebrated for the wrong reasons. It's often all about shopping, eating, and partying, and we forget why we celebrate Christmas in the first place.

Holidays and birthdays are wonderful times to remember how blessed we are. It's easy to take for granted all the things God has given us. We forget to consider the simple things, like a roof over our heads, food to eat, and a family surrounding us. We have so many blessings, and Christmas is a perfect time to show our thankfulness by giving to others.

When I was nineteen years old, I chose a family to bless for Christmas and gave the children and parents gifts. This tradition has become a way for me to share God's love during the holiday season. Even though the gifts are always appreciated, the act of giving those gifts is incredibly fulfilling. This is what Christmas is all about. It's a way to thank Jesus.

On Christmas and all throughout the year, let's give to genuinely show our gratitude as an act of worship. We should remember the greatest gift God gave us: the baby in the manger, the One the wise men bowed down before—our Savior.

PRAY

Faithful God, thank You for giving us Your Son. Thank You for how much You give me each day— the gift of Your unending love, the breath in my lungs, and the beauty of nature—and help me give generously to others. In Your Son's name, amen.

36

ENDURE IT

Don't worry about anything; instead, pray about
everything. Tell God what you need, and thank him for all
he has done. Then you will experience God's peace, which
exceeds anything we can understand. His peace will guard
your hearts and minds as you live in Christ Jesus.

—PHILIPPIANS 4:6–7

After my father passed away, I couldn't deny the pain I felt. There was a hole in my heart, a piece of me missing, an empty spot in my life. But there was Someone I did have— the Holy Spirit! The Spirit is able to fill our empty places. My spirit felt comforted knowing that Daddy was now in the presence of Jesus. It was what he had been preaching and teaching his whole life.

Stay at the feet of Jesus.

When something tragic happens, our lives can be flipped upside down. But in my grief, I discovered my foundation was more solid than I'd imagined. Our family's faith was stronger than I could have hoped for. We made it through my dad's passing because God held us in His hand. And this is true for you too.

When the darkness seeks to stamp out your light, go to the place where your flame can be reignited. When tragedy and disappointment threaten to rewrite the story God is telling through your life, run to the feet of the great author and perfecter of your faith.

The difficulties in our lives help us discover just how strong the Spirit is within us.

When stresses, troubles, and chaos show up, let Paul's words to the Philippians encourage you: Don't worry, but pray. Pray about everything. Share with God all the things you need, and praise Him for all He's done. Then you'll find the peace that passes all understanding.

Allow yourself to be strengthened by the example of Jesus. Remember His experience of enduring the cross and bearing its shame, and finally sitting at a place of honor beside God's throne.

> When you find yourselves flagging in your faith, go over that story again, item by item, that long litany of hostility he plowed through. *That* will shoot adrenaline into your souls! (Hebrews 12:3, MSG)

Whatever pain you might be enduring right now, God will give you the peace to make it through. If you feel stuck, God will urge you forward. If you feel heavy, God can lift your burden and make you feel light.

Don't give up hope. Look to Jesus! He reigns today!

PRAY

Gracious heavenly Lord, be with me today. Give me a peace that transcends thought and reason. Give me a spirit that settles the turmoil in my soul. Thank You for letting me run to You. In Jesus's name, amen.

37

EMBODY IT

We are God's masterpiece. He has created us anew in
Christ Jesus, so we can do the good things he planned for
us long ago.

—EPHESIANS 2:10

You are awesome. Do you believe it? You should. Not because I'm saying it, but because God's Word does.

"We are God's masterpiece."

Think about those four words. In the NIV translation, it says we are God's *handiwork*. The King James Version states that we are His *workmanship*. He transforms us into something remarkable, something that can do amazing things for Him.

God makes incredible things. In Scripture, the first trait we learn about our heavenly Father is that He is an artist. He created light and water and the sky and the seas. As God continued to establish the world and set up all the intricate forms of life, He saw that everything He made was good. But God's true masterpiece came when He created humankind.

That includes you and me.

Some days we might not feel like such a masterpiece. Maybe we realize how messy our lives are or how many times we've made mistakes. Maybe we compare ourselves with others. Whatever it might be, sometimes we wake up having lost sight of who we are in God's eyes.

Today, let's set the record straight in our own minds and join King David in saying, "Thank you for making me so wonderfully complex! Your workmanship is marvelous—how well I know it" (Psalm 139:14).

God knows *exactly* who He created you to be. Own your true identity! There is a freedom that comes with loving yourself and accepting who you are. Fight the pressure to compete and compare with others. Don't seek the validation of this world. Trust what God says about you and embody your value. Find rest in being *you*!

PRAY

Loving God, thank You for creating me. Thank You for every unique aspect of myself. Help me know every day that I am Your masterpiece. In Jesus's name, amen.

38

PROCLAIM IT

To keep me from becoming proud, I was given a thorn in my flesh, a messenger from Satan to torment me and keep me from becoming proud.

Three different times I begged the Lord to take it away. Each time he said, "My grace is all you need. My power works best in weakness." So now I am glad to boast about my weaknesses, so that the power of Christ can work through me.

—2 CORINTHIANS 12:7–9

"My grace is sufficient."[1]

We often hear this statement from 2 Corinthians, but we may forget the context in which it was written. The apostle Paul was writing to the Christians in Corinth and addressing the criticism he had received from those who questioned him as a leader. It wouldn't have been hard for Paul to defend himself—there were many things Paul could boast about—but in this passage he did the opposite. He shared that he was powerless in battling a thorn in his flesh and that he knew exactly why.

DO IT ANYWAY DEVOTIONAL

It was to keep him humble. To ensure he always stayed at the feet of Jesus.

We all have thorns in our flesh. It might be something significant, like an addictive trait. Or it may be a habit of choosing the wrong relationships. Whatever your thorn is, it's all too easy to let it dig into your soul. It's easy to beat yourself up with negative self-talk.

Why do I keep making the same mistake? Why can't I do better? I'm always going to fail . . .

Your weakness can lead you to a woeful place of depression. To a place where you feel defeated. You may even begin to believe that your thorn is too powerful to overcome.

But here's the reality: This isn't about the thorn at all. It's about you. And it's about God.

God allowed me to deal with my struggle with weight to perfect some things inside of me. For me, it wasn't *just* about food; it was about turning to something that's good in the moment but not good for me in the long run. This struggle helped me become more sharpened and disciplined in certain areas. It wasn't so much about a diet; it was about making good decisions.

Maybe that thorn in your flesh is there to keep you aligned with God's will for your life. To keep you humble. To keep you praying. To keep you dependent and knowing that you are nothing without God and His strength.

For whatever weakness you're dealing with, do what Paul did and celebrate it! Celebrate what God is doing in you through your weakness. Believe what He says about your weakness: "My power works best in weakness."

PRAY

Almighty God, help me acknowledge and accept my weaknesses. In Your grace, please bring me to Your feet so I can put these weaknesses before You. Thank You for letting the power of Christ work in me. In Jesus's name, amen.

39

ANTICIPATE IT

I don't think there's any comparison between the present hard times and the coming good times. The created world itself can hardly wait for what's coming next. Everything in creation is being more or less held back. God reins it in until both creation and all the creatures are ready and can be released at the same moment into the glorious times ahead. Meanwhile, the joyful anticipation deepens.

—ROMANS 8:18–21, MSG

Sometimes a passage of Scripture will snatch up my heart and make me want to praise Jesus! That's the case with today's verses. The words speak for themselves. When I read them, they wash redemption over my spirit.

Can you relate? Anybody can see that these present days are hard, but can you see the coming good times? The world is holding its breath and waiting for the glory ahead.

Let's not be full of anxiety. Let's be full of anticipation!

This waiting, Paul wrote, doesn't diminish us, but instead enlarges us like a pregnant mother. "The longer we wait, the larger we become, and the more joyful our expectancy" (Romans 8:25, MSG). God's Spirit helps us, especially when we grow weary of waiting.

If there is anything to remind us not to be uncertain about today but rather to focus on His glorious return, it's that Jesus knows exactly what we are going through. It doesn't matter if we don't know how to pray or what to pray, because Jesus is praying for us!

> He does our praying in and for us, making prayer out of our wordless sighs, our aching groans. He knows us far better than we know ourselves, knows our pregnant condition, and keeps us present before God. That's why we can be so sure that every detail in our lives of love for God is worked into something good. (verses 27–28, MSG)

Just think of the hope we have knowing Jesus is praying for us! That bright hope needs to shine throughout the dark days in our world.

Do you feel weary and run-down? Are you overwhelmed with the wickedness of our times or even the wickedness of your own heart?

Jesus knows, and He's praying for you.

From the very beginning of time, God has known what He is doing. If you love Him, He is shaping your life in ways you can't imagine. He is staying with you until the very end, until you and every believer bow before His throne.

PRAY

Holy God, thank You for Your words that speak hope daily into my life. Help me wait in anticipation for the wondrous and glorious hope that is mine with You in heaven. In Jesus's name, amen.

40

AVOID IT

*All Scripture is inspired by God and is useful to teach us
what is true and to make us realize what is wrong in our
lives. It corrects us when we are wrong and teaches us to
do what is right. God uses it to prepare and equip his
people to do every good work.*

—2 TIMOTHY 3:16–17

When I was in high school, I had a Ford Escort. It was a
beautiful car that I drove straight off the lot. I took good
care of that car, and the car took good care of me. But one
day, after I came home from college, I saw a gorgeous Isuzu
Trooper. It was sleek and shiny and glistened on the "Buy
Here Pay Here" car lot.

"Daddy, I want that car," I told my father.

My dad had already bought me the Ford Escort, and it
was still a perfect vehicle for me. But I had fallen in love
with that Isuzu Trooper and was relentless about trading in
the Escort.

"It's just so pretty," I told him. "And look—it's bigger.
Just come take a look at it with me. You're gonna fall in love
with it."

But even after my father went and sat in the Trooper, he didn't love it. In fact, he knew that the car was a piece of junk. After we got back home, Daddy tried to persuade me not to buy it. "Tasha, I think you should stick with the one you have. We can look for another car down the road."

"But it's a *limited*," I said. I was dying to get this car.

So Daddy let me trade in my Ford Escort for that hunk of junk that was a ticking bomb the moment I drove it off the lot. Why did he let me? Because he wanted me to learn something important. "Tasha—not all that is shiny in this world is what's best for you."

It didn't take long for me to learn that the Trooper I bought was a lemon. It broke down, and then it broke me down! Suddenly I was stuck with debt and no car.

My father was gracious. "Okay, baby, this is what Daddy's going to do. I need you to tell me what you've learned."

"Beware of those shiny things in life that we don't need."

He helped me get rid of the Trooper and start over with a brand-new car. He made sure we got a car that would take me through the next season of life.

My dad allowed me to learn that lesson even though it was tough on him. God does the same with us. Sometimes God will walk us through something uncomfortable so we'll learn a lesson that will guide us well for a lifetime.

What shiny things in your life have you chased after only to learn a hard truth? What shiny things do you need to avoid today?

PRAY

Gracious God, thank You for the lessons You teach me. Thank You for loving me enough to guide my path and for helping me after I make mistakes. In Jesus's name, amen.

41

LIVE IT

*If any of you wants to be my follower, you must give up
your own way, take up your cross daily, and follow me.*

—LUKE 9:23

I love Sunday mornings. Surrounded by sisters and brothers in Christ, worshipping in song and in spirit, glorifying God and feeling His presence, becoming inspired and ignited. But then comes Monday morning. Back to normal.

I've learned to view Sunday mornings in the same way I view my performances: What we do on the stage is a small percentage of what worship truly is. Worship is how we live from Monday to Saturday as well. How do you treat people each day? How do you represent Christ in your home to your spouse and children? How do you navigate the stresses and struggles of everyday life? Those things are just as important as getting on a stage and singing a song. In fact, it's out of the context of our week that our Sunday-morning worship flows.

I cannot be as effective on the stage if I'm not submitted and committed to the walk of worship in my everyday life. That includes reading the Word of God and keeping it in my heart. It means praying and having a consistent conversation with Him, and asking Him what His will is for my life. The same is true for you: You will not be as effective in your mission (whatever that looks like for you in this season) if you're not committed to worshipping throughout your week.

Do you struggle with this? Do you find yourself thinking that worship is only a Sunday sort of thing? Do you put God on the shelf Monday through Saturday?

Worship is about the posture of your heart. Yes, Sundays are important. Hebrews 10:25 says, "Let us not neglect our meeting together, as some people do, but encourage one another." Gathering with our brothers and sisters is a source of strength, accountability, belonging, and love. But a worshipful posture of our heart needs to be lived out the rest of the week. It's about giving God those Monday-morning blues, keeping steadfast in the Word through Wednesday, and truly thanking God it's Friday!

How are you living out your relationship with Christ Monday through Saturday?

PRAY

Dear Lord God, thank You that You are the same every day and that You invite me to come before You at all times. Help me worship You daily. In Jesus's name, amen.

42

REALIZE IT

*My sheep listen to my voice; I know them, and they
follow me.*

—JOHN 10:27

Even before Kenny and I were married, we were mentors.
We both shared a desire to help people find their purpose
and walk it out. I've always wanted to encourage people
toward their full potential, to pray with them, and to get
them to consider what God wants to do with their lives. I've
always loved to sing and worship, but I also love seeing
people grow and become better at what they're called to do.
This is one of my greatest joys in life.

I believe that before we enter this earth, God places an
assignment on each of our lives. He gives us a purpose. Yet
until we realize and trust what that purpose is, we resemble
nomads, trying to figure it out. *Is this me? Or is that me?* A
lot of our identity crises arise when we don't know who we
are and what our purpose is.

Faith in God involves discovering the purpose He has
given us. We might even be living it out without knowing it!
Seek the Lord and He will reveal it to you. As Jeremiah 29:11

says, "'For I know the plans I have for you,' says the LORD. 'They are plans for good and not for disaster, to give you a future and a hope.'"

Are you still looking for your purpose? Are you discovering this joy I'm talking about? It starts with beginning each day seeking God. Ask Him what He wants out of your life. But to hear that, you have to be close to Him. You have to be listening and walking alongside Him.

A friend once told me that if you're struggling to hear God and feel Him near, simply begin by studying the Gospels.

When I asked him why, he said, "Because you act like who you hang out with. And if you study the Gospels, you're walking with Jesus every day."

If you've never read the Gospels, then you can't expect to act like Jesus Christ or to know your true purpose. So begin that walk. Start in Matthew, move on to Mark, and then Luke, and finally John. By the time you get to the end of John, you will be closer to knowing your true purpose. You'll better understand what God has planned for your life.

"Jesus spoke to the people once more and said, 'I am the light of the world. If you follow me, you won't have to walk in darkness, because you will have the light that leads to life'" (John 8:12).

PRAY

Loving God, speak to me and tell me what You want from my life. Help me find my place, realize my purpose on this earth, and live it out with boldness. Thank You that I can walk with You every day. In Jesus's name, amen.

43

CELEBRATE IT

There are different kinds of service, but the same Lord.
There are different kinds of working, but in all of them
and in everyone it is the same God at work.

—I CORINTHIANS 12:5–6, NIV

Science has proven that sounds can shatter glass. We can experience that to an extent when the booming bass in a car causes everything to vibrate. Or when the television is blaring and it causes some things to rumble. With the right volume and the right frequency, a human voice can indeed break glass.[1]

Have I ever witnessed this personally? No—not yet! But I've seen it happen from a spiritual standpoint every time I sing. In the same way sound has a physical power in it, I believe it has an even stronger power when God is behind it. Songs can spiritually shatter things and put them back in order. I've watched how songs move hearts. They can inspire worship. They can spark a newfound passion for the Lord. All this is possible when God is working through the musical gift He's given me.

I'm blessed to be able to use my voice to encourage others. But I know music isn't birthed in vocal cords; it comes from the soul, from the place of our emotion and passion. God gave me this gift, but not for myself. He gave it to me so I can share it with others. I know when I lift my voice, God is going to show up and make something happen.

What gifts did God give you? Yours may not be the same as mine. God gives us all different gifts. What do *you* do best?

Thank God for those gifts! Celebrate them!

Now consider how you can use your gift to encourage someone else. To build a bridge to them. To get them to think about heaven. To allow God to stir their heart.

Give your gifts and talents to God. Place them at the feet of Jesus.

When you have boldness in those gifts He has given you, God will use them in ways that shatter limitations and lies, and will reveal His love and life to those who see your work on display!

PRAY

Heavenly Father, thank You for making me unique and giving me talents and abilities. Help me recognize them and celebrate them. Help me surrender them to You so You can use them for Your glory. In Jesus's name, amen.

44

CURSE IT

You have not received a spirit that makes you fearful
slaves. Instead, you received God's Spirit when he
adopted you as his own children. Now we call him,
"Abba, Father." For his Spirit joins with our spirit to
affirm that we are God's children. And since we are his
children, we are his heirs. In fact, together with Christ we
are heirs of God's glory. But if we are to share his glory,
we must also share his suffering.

—ROMANS 8:15–17

Years ago, I struggled through a season of deep depression. At the time, God was opening doors for me and was letting me use my gift of worship to help and heal others. I was ministering to churches and seeing people experience freedom, but then I would go home and be imprisoned by darkness once again.

The pain surrounded me, and I would be bound for days at a time. I was isolated and alone and feeling plagued by heaviness.

Have you been there? We all have dark days. Days when

we're down-and-out. Days when we're shackled by doubt. Maybe the dark days come and go, or maybe you're there right now.

In my dark midnight, God spoke to my heart.

Get up, Tasha. Get up and study the spirit of rejection. You've been calling this depression, but your depression grows from the root of rejection.

I started studying the Scriptures, and I also sought help from others. What I discovered was that the darkness eclipsing my soul was attached to this sense of rejection buried inside. I knew I had to work through it—and that it would take some time. But I began by making a vow to God every morning. I looked in the mirror and made the following declaration: "I curse the spirit of rejection, and I receive the spirit of adoption."

I said it every single day. Slowly but surely God allowed me to reclaim my joy and to renew my life.

Do you feel rejection in your life? Or anxiety? Or unworthiness? Do you feel like you're wandering without purpose? Do you wade through life bound by your mistakes?

Don't give up. There's hope for you right now. Curse the spirit of rejection or the spirit of fear. Curse whatever spirit is breaking you because those spirits are not from God.

Instead, receive the spirit of adoption.

You are not alone.

You have been chosen by God.

He adopted you as His own.

You belong to God.

PRAY

Merciful Savior, thank You for adopting me as Your child. Thank You for saving me and for delivering me. Forgive me of my sins. I praise Your holy name. In Jesus's name, amen.

45

SHINE IT

Let your light so shine before men, that they may see your good works, and glorify your Father which is in heaven.

—MATTHEW 5:16, KJV

We all tend to show ourselves in the best light possible, especially on social media. And so many people *love* to let their light shine before everyone, but not in the way Jesus described in today's verse from the Sermon on the Mount. We love to show the best parts of our lives—the highlight reels and the happy moments. It's easy to make it about ourselves and leave God out of the picture.

I believe that social media exposes the heart of people. Sometimes we really are what we "post" to be! Nowadays, everyone has a platform to express their opinions—and that's not always a bad thing. Unfortunately, we live in a society of people who post words or images or videos that belittle others to make themselves feel better and cover their own insecurities. It's easy to be pulled in by this negativity. We laugh at it or affirm it, or we engage in a pointless debate with the stranger who posted it.

What we need to do is reflect the light of Christ, the true light of this world! With so much hate and anger making people feel like giving up, we need to share how God is still moving in our world for His people.

I've experienced my own share of backlash and criticism on social media, so I'm sensitive to others who receive or fear harsh negativity. No one should be bullied, online or face-to-face. But instead of spending our energy worrying about haters and instigators, we should look at Jesus's example. Throughout His life, people were bad-mouthing Him, questioning Him, lying about Him, and even trying to kill Him! So if anyone understands how to deal with the negativity, it's Him. Surely, with His help, we can follow His example.

Most of us are striving to do better today than we did yesterday, whether that's with our family and friends or in the way we show up in the world. We long to represent Christ well.

I love how *The Message* translation phrases today's passage:

Here's another way to put it: You're here to be light, bringing out the God-colors in the world. God is not a secret to be kept. We're going public with this, as public as a city on a hill. If I make you light-bearers, you don't think I'm going to hide you under a bucket, do you? I'm putting you on a light stand. Now that I've put you there on a hilltop, on a light stand— shine! Keep open house; be generous with your lives.

By opening up to others, you'll prompt people to open up with God, this generous Father in heaven. (Matthew 5:14–16)

Don't let anything dim God's light in you.

PRAY

Dear Lord God, please forgive me for not sharing the light You gave me. Give me the boldness to confess Your name and shine Your light online, face-to-face, and in every place I can. In Jesus's name, amen.

46

ACCOMPLISH IT

Whatever you do or say, do it as a representative of the
Lord Jesus, giving thanks through him to God the Father.

—COLOSSIANS 3:17

"Woo! Come on—clap your hands! God's gonna get the glory."

As I began to sing on the stage at the magical Ryman Auditorium in Nashville, I knew we were making history as the first Christian gospel worship album that had ever been recorded in this historic Nashville building. The stage was set, the lights were primed, the sound was dialed in.

"You're gonna get the glory out of this!" I sang in this auditorium . . . to an audience of one.

We had prepared and planned and marketed for this concert, but then the pandemic hit and everything was put on pause. It was devastating to think the concert wouldn't happen, so Kenny and I prayed about it and God gave me an answer.

They might be shutting down the world, but they can't shut
down worshipping God!

We were going to do it anyway!

So in a building that only allowed twenty-five people, I praised God to rows of empty seats.

"I don't need to understand," I sang. "God, I trust Your plan."

My first Ryman appearance—and nobody was in the room! Only Tasha. But this was beautiful and brilliant because it was an opportunity to demonstrate what we as worship leaders often say: We have an audience of one. And that day, I *literally* had an audience of One: my Lord and Savior.

"I know You're using this," I sang.[1]

This was an opportunity to spread good news and inspiration to people as the performance was recorded and streamed. It was an honor to be there in this theater to sing about God and give Him glory. And I knew that people didn't need to be in the room for this to speak to them. God was going to use this—and is *still* using it—for His glory!

We may not always have an audience, yet our work can give God the glory. No one sees us quietly praying for others in the early hours of the morning; no one sees us cooking another dinner for our family; no one may know all the sweat we poured into our work project. But that doesn't matter, because when God gives us an opportunity to worship Him in any capacity, we need to do it without hesitation. We don't need a stage, and we don't need a standing ovation.

God's hand is moving in every situation. So don't stop worshipping Him. Don't stop working to do good. And don't stop spreading the good news and encouraging others in any way you can.

PRAY

Loving God, thank You for seeing every minute of my life. Help me never hesitate to take any opportunity to be a blessing to others. Give me the boldness to carry out Your mission in my life—whether others see it or not. All the glory is Yours. In Jesus's name, amen.

47

OVERCOME IT

When you go through deep waters,
  I will be with you.
When you go through rivers of difficulty,
  you will not drown.
When you walk through the fire of oppression,
  you will not be burned up;
  the flames will not consume you.

—ISAIAH 43:2

Isaiah tells us that even when we're facing the strongest hardship, God is near us. He is there to protect us and to comfort us.

I felt lost in my own river of difficulty leading up to the live recording at the Ryman. I grasped on to God for His comfort. I needed a lot of it.

For several years, Kenny and I had been going through a season of infertility where we were praying and asking God to bless us. We were trusting God's plan and working through an IVF process. But three days before the concert, doctors told us that we had lost the baby.

Despite the grief, we continued to do the work God wanted us to do. That concert before an audience of One wasn't just a performance; those songs were an act of worship drawn from real hardship. Nobody except God and Kenny knew that I was standing there on stage with an elastic bandage to help with the physical pain I was feeling. Still, I praised God, knowing He was in control, knowing He knew what I was going through.

"I'm healed, I'm healed!"[1] I declared over myself that night.

Moments like this are when God wants us to come to His feet, to let Him lead us.

I'm encouraged by Paul's words in 2 Corinthians 4:16–18:

That is why we never give up. Though our bodies are dying, our spirits are being renewed every day. For our present troubles are small and won't last very long. Yet they produce for us a glory that vastly outweighs them and will last forever! So we don't look at the troubles we can see now; rather, we fix our gaze on things that cannot be seen. For the things we see now will soon be gone, but the things we cannot see will last forever.

Never give up. Fix your gaze beyond your troubles and on God and His sovereignty. Notice how God's comfort surrounds you even now. Just as He promised, He will sustain you. You will overcome!

PRAY

Dear heavenly Father, I praise You for how You care for me during my most difficult times. In times of fear and anxiety, remind me of Your presence and provision. Fill me with Your hopeful Spirit today. In Jesus's name, amen.

48

SILENCE IT

You're hopeless, you religion scholars and Pharisees!
Frauds! You keep meticulous account books, tithing on
every nickel and dime you get, but on the meat of God's
Law, things like fairness and compassion and
commitment— the absolute basics!—you carelessly take
it or leave it.

—MATTHEW 23:23, MSG

John 3 tells the story of a Pharisee who secretly went to
Jesus at night to ask Him questions. This wasn't just any
ordinary Pharisee; Nicodemus was a member of the Sanhe-
drin, which served as the elite Jewish court (think the Su-
preme Court for Israel at that time).¹ Many people, including
Nicodemus, were impressed by Jesus's miracles, but they
weren't necessarily interested in His message.

The Pharisees knew *too much*. They had way too much
information.

They were impressed by Jesus's wonders and signs but
not by His presence.

Let's be honest: In this age of knowledge and information, we aren't that far removed from this. If we are not

careful, we, too, will find ourselves seeking signs, miracles, and wonders more than we seek Jesus's presence. We have access to so much information, yet we are impressed by *so little*!

It's similar to when your children say those two most ridiculous words in today's culture: "I'm bored."

They have every kind of video game at their disposal and every known app on their devices. They have so many ways to communicate and to express themselves. They can explore whatever they want with the click of a button. Yet they're still bored!

It's a reflection of human nature.

We're overstimulated. We know too much and yet we apply so little.

Perhaps we have so much noise in our lives that we can't recognize when God is present in the stillness.

Even amid the noise of Nicodemus's life, the Pharisee met with Jesus face-to-face while his peers didn't. He didn't encounter a man claiming to be God but rather God who had come down to earth in the form of a man. When we meet with Jesus, our desire should not be to simply gather more information on life but to look Him in the eyes and actually meet with the divine, holy God.

Do you struggle to hear from God? Do you feel exhausted by all the things that clamor for your attention? Find a way to go before the presence of God and listen for Him. Find that one place with Jesus where everything else is silenced.

PRAY

Dear gracious Lord, thank You for making sense of all the information around me and helping me remember what is true and important. Drown out the noise in my life. Wash over the information I have in my head and cleanse me. Give me the boldness and wisdom to live out the truths You've taught me. I ask in Jesus's name, amen.

49

TRUST IT

Don't let your hearts be troubled. Trust in God, and trust also in me. There is more than enough room in my Father's home. If this were not so, would I have told you that I am going to prepare a place for you?

—JOHN 14:1–2

When Jesus told His disciples that He wouldn't be with them much longer, they grew deeply disturbed. They were confused. Where was Jesus going? Why would He leave them?

So Jesus spoke words for all of us: "Don't let your hearts be troubled. Trust in God, and trust also in me."

So much of the strength and depth of our relationship with God is about trust. The boldness with which we live out our faith comes down to trust.

God tells us, *Still your heart and trust in Me.*

Moses told the Israelites in Exodus 14:13: "Don't be afraid. Just stand still and watch the LORD rescue you today."

A year after my father died, I did an interview and someone brought up his passing. The interviewer surprised me by what he said. "We are so proud of how your family ex-emplified how Christians are supposed to grieve."

I had never thought about that. It's easy to teach and preach about how God is our peace, but there are times when we have to live that out in front of the world. What happens when our only source of peace really is the Lord? In front of a watching world, we made the decision to run to Jesus's feet.

Still, it's easy to forget. Even the disciples forgot the words of Isaiah 9:6:

> For a child is born to us,
>   a son is given to us. . . .
>   And he will be called:
> Wonderful Counselor, Mighty God,
>   Everlasting Father, Prince of Peace.

God tells us, "I am the Prince of Peace. *Trust Me.*"

God is in control. He was in control when He hung on a cross. And He was in control when He rose from the grave.

I pray that today your heart is still and your fears are calmed and that you can sing Isaiah 40:31 in your soul:

> They that wait upon the LORD shall renew their strength; they shall mount up with wings as eagles; they shall run, and not be weary; and they shall walk, and not faint. (KJV)

Keep the faith! Don't ever let the powers of darkness overshadow the Prince of Peace.

PRAY

Dear gracious Lord, thank You for being the God who brings me peace. Help me remember, in the easy days and the difficult days, that You are trustworthy. Forgive me for not trusting You more. Give me the peace I need to glorify You today. In Jesus's name, amen.

50

LEAVE IT

Soon a fierce storm came up. High waves were breaking into the boat, and it began to fill with water.

Jesus was sleeping at the back of the boat with his head on a cushion. The disciples woke him up, shouting, "Teacher, don't you care that we're going to drown?"

When Jesus woke up, he rebuked the wind and said to the waves, "Silence! Be still!" Suddenly the wind stopped, and there was a great calm. Then he asked them, "Why are you afraid? Do you still have no faith?"

The disciples were absolutely terrified. "Who is this man?" they asked each other. "Even the wind and waves obey him!"

—MARK 4:37–41

With the waters raging around them, the disciples were terrified for their lives. Jesus simply told the storm to silence and be still, and that was that. The tempest disappeared.

Afterward, Jesus didn't send His disciples away in anger. Instead, He asked them why they were afraid. After all this time, they were struggling to fully believe in Him.

Do you spend too much of your day listening to those noisy and violent storms of social media? The vicious and unrelenting howls online? The criticism, the hate, and the evil that never go away? Do you get caught up in debates and arguments and wade around in cynicism? Is it difficult to truly hear from God?

Jesus can quiet those storms too.

In 1 Kings 19, the prophet Elijah went up on the mountain to hear God speak to him. A mighty windstorm blew through the mountain, ripping the rocks loose. But Elijah didn't hear God's voice. Then a violent earthquake rumbled, but God wasn't in the earthquake. A fire ravaged the mountain, but still Elijah did not hear the Lord. And then he heard the sound of a gentle whisper.

It was God, speaking to the prophet in the peaceful stillness.

There are times when we need to take a break from the online tempests and listen for God's whisper in the stillness. There are other times we need to put our full faith in Jesus and ask Him to quiet a particular storm in our lives. Maybe it's a difficult relationship or a stressful work situation or an insurmountable to-do list. Whatever it might be, we can ask God to quiet the winds and waves of our lives!

Jesus can quiet all storms.

PRAY

Heavenly Father, I praise You for being in control of everything in this world. Thank You for delivering me from the storms that come in my life. Help me listen for You in this noisy world. In Jesus's name, amen.

51

FACE IT

A giant nearly ten feet tall stepped out from the Philistine line into the open, Goliath from Gath. He had a bronze helmet on his head and was dressed in armor—126 pounds of it! He wore bronze shin guards and carried a bronze sword. His spear was like a fence rail—the spear tip alone weighed over fifteen pounds. His shield bearer walked ahead of him.

—1 SAMUEL 17:4–7, MSG

The story of David and Goliath is one of those all-time great stories, whether you're a Christian or a non-believer who just happened to hear it. I can imagine the scene on the battlefield between the Israelites and the Philistines. I appreciate how much detail is given to Goliath's introduction in the verses above.

Imagine that poor shield bearer lugging the massive shield and thinking, *How'd I end up with this job?* Now picture Goliath shouting to the Israelites, daring them to send their best fighter to face him. And here comes innocent David from tending his flock of sheep to bring the Israelite soldiers some food. He finds a whole army full of frightened warriors and he can't believe it.

"Who does the giant think he is to taunt the armies of God?" David says.[1]

When his big brother hears what he's saying, he tells him to mind his own business and go back home. But David refuses. When the Israelite king hears what David is saying, he sends for him.

"Master, don't give up hope," David tells King Saul. "Send me in to fight the giant."

It takes David a while to convince the king, but he does. I wonder what everyone was thinking when they watched David step onto the battlefield. They were probably looking away, preparing for the worst. *That poor shepherd's gone crazy. He's spent too much time around his sheep!* But young, inexperienced David isn't afraid.

Soldiers on the field have the right equipment and the right training, but David bypasses all of this. He stands firm on two things: his history that God has come through before when he had to fight a lion and a bear, and his relationship with God.

David believes, *I might not be strong enough to do this, but God's going to give me the strength to do it.*

The rest is epic and breathtaking. Goliath laughs and mocks and brags about what he can do. But David believes and stands firm and declares that there's an extraordinary God in Israel. "The battle belongs to GOD—he's handing you to us on a platter!" (1 Samuel 17:47, MSG).

You know what happens next. Goliath charges. David

puts a stone in his sling, swings it around, and whips it at the giant's head. *Boom.* Just like that.

If David was holding a microphone, this would be the moment for him to look around at all the soldiers and then drop it.

We all know and love this story, yet how often do we forget about it when it comes to the giants in our own lives? I know you have at least one giant. I have two—my mental health and my weight issues. But I don't battle those by myself.

How many times have you dealt with something in your life that has you saying, *Oh my God, this is going to take me out. I'm never going to overcome this.*

Some victories do not look like instantaneous miracles. For some people, their giants may be a fight with emotions or mental stability. Some giants meet us on the battlefield every day. There are times we have to make better or even drastic choices in order to overcome our giants.

We all face some type of giant. Scripture talks about a thorn in our flesh,[2] which is a nagging reminder that we're human, weaker than we want to be, and that we're going to have to work our entire lives on some struggles. We might not be strong enough to defeat it—we might not even be strong enough to *face* it—but God will give us the strength to do it. Remember David and stand on those two things: God always comes through in one way or another. And being in a relationship with Him gives us the strength to defeat our giants.

PRAY

Dear God, thank You for controlling everything in this world, including what happens inside and around me. Thank You for defeating the giants in my life. Give me the strength I need today to step onto any battlefield knowing You stand with me. In Jesus's name, amen.

52

ENCOURAGE IT

*I am giving you a sign of my covenant with you and with
all living creatures, for all generations to come. I have
placed my rainbow in the clouds. It is the sign of my
covenant with you and with all the earth.*

—GENESIS 9:12–13

We all need encouragement, especially during the difficult
seasons of life. While it takes a lot of work to be faithful and
patient—and remember that God has everything under
control—it also takes a lot of work to encourage others to
do the same. Often, we hesitate to even ask how someone is
doing because we're worried about not having the right response. We remain silent, plagued by doubts.

What if I give them the wrong advice?

How can I ever relate to their situation?

*I want to be sensitive and respectful, so what if I say some-
thing trite?*

More than having the perfect words to say, real encouragement is drawn from true words. God's promises are
never trite or fake. They are real, and they are true. Paul

wrote, "This same God who takes care of me will supply all your needs from his glorious riches, which have been given to us in Christ Jesus" (Philippians 4:19).

I love this quote from Maya Angelou's book *Letter to My Daughter:*

> You may not control all the events that happen to you, but you can decide not to be reduced by them. Try to be a rainbow in someone's cloud. Do not complain. Make every effort to change things you do not like. If you cannot make a change, change the way you have been thinking. You might find a new solution.[1]

As I wrote in my song "Gotta Believe," there truly is a rainbow behind the clouds. And the rainbow is a promise that God made to all of us. It is the first covenant God gave to mankind.

> When I send clouds over the earth, the rainbow will appear in the clouds, and I will remember my covenant with you and with all living creatures. Never again will the floodwaters destroy all life. (Genesis 9:14–15)

This was God's expression of grace and a promise of His constant provision.

When we are waiting on God, we need to look to the sky and believe. And when others are desperate and in need of hope, we can point them to the promise of the rainbow and to the good grace that God gives us all.

PRAY

Almighty God, I praise You for Your grace and mercy. Thank You for all You have created. Help me be an encourager to others in my life who need Your love. In Jesus's name, amen.

53

REMEMBER IT

*After this, Jesus, knowing that all things were now
accomplished, that the Scripture might be fulfilled, said,
"I thirst!" Now a vessel full of sour wine was sitting
there; and they filled a sponge with sour wine, put it on
hyssop, and put it to His mouth. So when Jesus had
received the sour wine, He said, "It is finished!" And
bowing His head, He gave up His spirit.*

—JOHN 19:28–30, NKJV

The cross is the symbol of Christianity. It stands on top of churches, hangs in front of sanctuaries, and dangles from necklaces. But those who lived during the time of the Roman Empire never would have imagined that such a thing would be immortalized like this.

For them, the cross was a symbol of horrific suffering.

Crucifixion was a method of execution that had been around since before the Romans, but they perfected it. During the time of Christ, it was common to see crosses on the side of the roads leading into the cities with the dead and the dying hanging on them. The cross was a very public reminder of the power of the Roman Empire.

We tend to forget about the true pain and suffering that Jesus went through as He was crucified. He hung on the cross by the long spikes driven through His wrists. Nails also impaled His feet. Execution by crucifixion was designed to last for days. Most of the time victims slowly suffocated while in excruciating pain.

It's difficult and uncomfortable to fully grasp the scope of Jesus's suffering on Calvary's hill, but that's exactly what we must acknowledge to understand what our Savior did.

Jesus endured this despicable public display of agony for us.

Jesus bore our shame so that we could be granted mercy.

Jesus died so that we can live.

Everything we need is there at the cross. This is the place we need to go again and again. To remember His suffering.

"It is finished!" Jesus said while on the cross.[1]

His mission was accomplished. The sacrifice was done. His redemption was complete. The cross reminds us that Jesus finished His work. Salvation is ready and available for all who come before Him.

We must never forget the gruesome scene at Calvary. But we must also remember that Jesus's death was not the end of the story but the beginning. Jesus conquered death! He rose again! That's why we now celebrate the Cross. He rescues all who come before Him.

What an incredible Savior is our God and King!

PRAY

Dear loving God, thank You for sending Your Son to die on the cross for me! Thank You for forgiving my sins that Jesus bore. I praise You and thank You for Your powerful love for me. In Jesus's name, amen.

54

HOLD IT

Truly I tell you, today you will be with me in paradise.

—LUKE 23:43, NIV

There is no heart that isn't loved by Jesus. And there is no expiration date for when salvation can be received.

As Jesus suffered on the cross to pay the ultimate price for our sins, on each side of Him hung a criminal being crucified as well.

One of the criminals hanging alongside cursed him: "Some Messiah you are! Save yourself! Save us!"

But the other one made him shut up: "Have you no fear of God? You're getting the same as him. We deserve this, but not him—he did nothing to deserve this."[1]

This criminal surely knew about Jesus. He knew Jesus was innocent. And in this moment, he believed that Jesus was the Son of God, that He was going to be raised from the dead, and that He would forgive everyone who confessed His name.

This guilty man cried out to his guiltless Savior. "Jesus, remember me when you enter your kingdom."[2]

Despite His agony, suffering, and shame, Jesus gave the criminal the same grace He gives us all.

"Don't worry, I will. Today you will join me in paradise."[3]

We don't know how much longer that criminal lived, but it wasn't very long. After a life of living for himself and living in a world of sin, the man found redemption.

In that moment, one of His final acts, Jesus gave life to another even as He was dying.

Jesus saves.

"I was living in a world of sin, and if He saved me, He can do it for you."[4]

Salvation is free to everyone who believes.

Maybe you have family members or friends who turned their backs on God many years ago and have made their lives a colossal mess. Maybe you work with people who love this wicked world. But remember something: There is no place too far for God's love to reach! Don't count anyone as too far gone.

Belief is a beautiful thing, especially coming from a broken soul. Jesus forgives everyone who comes to Him and cries out to be saved. We need to hold on to this eternal hope, especially in this heartless world. Never give up on anybody, because Christ never gave up on you.

PRAY

Savior God, I give You praise and glory for what You did at Calvary. Thank You for never giving up on me, no matter what I do. Forgive me for not always seeing the hope and opportunities in others who don't know You. Help me be bold in reaching out to these people in my life for Your sake. In Jesus's name, amen.

55

RECLAIM IT

I tell you the truth, unless you are born again, you cannot see the Kingdom of God.

—JOHN 3:3

As the ten-year anniversary of my first album approached, my label wanted to remaster and rerelease it. I went back and listened to it, and when I revisited the song "Your Heart"—particularly the lyrics "I want your heart, nothing else matters Lord"—one thought came to my mind: *I miss this innocence.*

There was a purity in this album and in these songs, one that came from innocence. I had little experience or information about the music industry back then. And to be honest, as I listened to the album, I became a little grieved in my spirit about whether I could get that innocence back. Too many things had happened. I'd had too many conversations, experiences, and disappointments. So I prayed to God to get that innocence back, and He reminded me of what Jesus told Nicodemus: "I tell you the truth, unless you are born again, you cannot see the Kingdom of God."

When Nicodemus asked Jesus to explain the meaning of this, Jesus went one step further.

> Very truly I tell you, no one can enter the kingdom of God unless they are born of water and the Spirit. (verse 5, NIV)

What did Jesus mean by "water"? Water symbolizes cleansing. I realized that Jesus was saying that the cleansing process of being born again isn't a one-time thing. We must be cleansed again every day. We must do it again and again and again. But we can't do it ourselves. This is something that can only come from God.

That's why we need to run to Jesus *daily*. He helps us properly filter those life experiences that try to dilute our anointing. The culture we live in, the industry we work in, the abuse, betrayal, and disappointment we've suffered at the hands of others—coming to the feet of Jesus helps us deal with those experiences that weigh us down and distort our vision. Jesus cleanses and heals our hearts; He restores our innocence.

Every day, we have a chance to be made new again. And that's by coming to the Lord and asking for forgiveness for our sins and believing that He can renew our faith.

PRAY

Heavenly Father, help me find my innocence once more today. Give me the desire to want Your heart and to know that nothing else matters. In Jesus's name, amen.

56

REACH IT

I am giving you a new commandment: Love each other.
Just as I have loved you, you should love each other.

—JOHN 13:34

My father left me a mantra. He instilled in me two things. All throughout this devotional, I've shared how he always told me to stay at the feet of Jesus. But he also taught me to love everybody. That was his thing. My father was one of the kindest and most loving people you would ever meet. He was truly a man after God's heart. At the end of each of our worship services, he would instruct the congregation, "Love everybody."

There was another lesson he laid out for me. But this came from his actions, not his words.

If my dad were alive right now, he would be a super entrepreneur. But when he was growing up, people weren't cultivating young black men to launch into the world of entrepreneurship. My father was a carpenter who was always building things in his free time. I went to school one day and came home to find that he had built an addition onto our house! He was a creator, an innovator. So when he passed away, I decided I wanted I celebrate his life and legacy in a special way by launching Fritz Eyewear Collection, named after Daddy.

I didn't know anything about this entrepreneurial world, but it didn't stop me. After spending a year educating myself on eyewear and working on building a line, we were ready to launch the Fritz Eyewear Collection with four amazing frames. Since my father was a living and breathing example of God's love on this earth, I wanted the people who wore these frames to literally see the world and people the way my father did—through the lens of love!

A year later, God validated this new enterprise when I attended an eyewear expo in Las Vegas. We had a small booth in the middle of this massive arena where thousands of people had gathered.

As soon as I stepped foot on the floor, a man spotted me and rushed over to greet me. "I never thought I'd meet you!" He explained with delight and tears how much I had inspired him.

The Holy Spirit immediately revealed something very important to me. *Not everyone will come to your church, Tasha. You've got to go to them!*

My encouragement to you is not just to take bold leaps of faith in your life but to remember that there are so many people who aren't comfortable coming to church. There are people who don't want to be involved with ministry or don't know what the term *worship* even means. But God loves them the same way He loves us. We need to show those people the same kind of love my father showed so many.

That means we have to go and reach out to them!

How can you step outside of your comfort zone to reach people who don't know the hope Jesus offers? Can you use your passions and your dreams to show love to others?

Who is God moving you toward? Not only do we need to hold open the doors of our church to welcome fellow believers, but we also need to walk through doors we never knew existed to share God's love with others.

PRAY

Dear heavenly Father, I praise You for all the people You have put in my life who have shown me how to love others the way You love us. Help me today to show this love to people who don't know You. In Jesus's name, amen.

57

BREAK IT

He brought them out of darkness, the utter darkness,
and broke away their chains.

—PSALM 107:14, NIV

God grants every single one of us a calling and a purpose.
That is what He desires for us.

As His children, we are charged to maximize our potential here on earth. But sometimes before we can walk out
purpose, we need to be sifted. And believe me, being sifted
by God can really sting!

During those days when I was suffering in silence with
anxiety and stress, God needed to break something inside of
me so that I could become the woman He wanted me to be.
He communicated with me in the best way He could:
through a song. It was late at night when I was driving my
team for hours and I heard the song "Break Every Chain"
for the first time.

Tears of release began to flow. Something deep inside of
me broke open. The walls I had built up inside began to
crumble. The mask I had been wearing for many years sud-

denly began to dissolve. This song ministered to me and allowed the Holy Spirit to speak to my heart.

Tasha, you're on a path to major things, but there's something standing in the way that you've got to allow Me to break.

I knew that in order to move to the next place God wanted me to be, I needed to embrace the message of that song.

How could I show others the power of Jesus's name when I felt powerless myself?

How could I help raise an army when I felt lower and lower with each passing day?

God broke the chains of darkness and despair. That song helped me experience deliverance and true healing.

I've never grown tired of singing "Break Every Chain," because there's always someone who needs it. They don't need the song's melody; they need the message.

Even as believers striving to follow Jesus, too many of us live our lives shackled by fears and frustration. We trudge along carrying the pain of our past instead of sprinting toward the future God wants for us.

Do you have chains that need to be broken? Do you have the weight of this world keeping you stuck in place? Pray right now and ask God to snap those chains in half!

PRAY

Dear gracious Lord, thank You for the power You give me. I praise You for Your love and Your mercy. Please break the chains the Enemy has placed around me. Help me be a light for You in this dark world. In Jesus's name, amen.

58

CRAVE IT

Open my eyes that I may see
wonderful things in your law.

—PSALM 119:18, NIV

"Now behold the Lamb. The Precious Lamb of God."[1]

With my eyes shut and the youth choir next to me, I sang the song in front of the packed church. I never wanted to be put in this position, but God had other plans.

I was fifteen years old and full of fear. I finally finished the song and opened my eyes. When I saw the reaction of the people in the pews—the tears and the glorious worship—I realized something: I had found my calling.

That vivid moment when I first led an audience into worship changed everything in my life. I use it to illustrate what happens when *God* opens our eyes. When we see the profound truths presented in the Bible, a veil is lifted and we are able to visualize new and amazing things. It's like a bright light suddenly being turned on in a pitch-black basement.

More often than we think, God is in the business of

opening our eyes to His wisdom and insight. He can reveal His truths wherever we go throughout the day, and He *consistently* opens our eyes through His Word.

When you hold your Bible, you hold the mysteries of the universe in your hand. Picture the power of the almighty Creator on the pages in front of you. The Word of God is full of wonder and revelation.

When we have a relationship with Christ, the Scriptures become more than simple words and principles. It's one thing to have a set of rules to live by. But without sitting at the feet of Jesus, the wisdom in the Holy Word is merely a set of principles. Sitting at His feet invokes God's presence in our lives, and His presence can do what my presence will never be able to do.

When was the last time your eyes were opened? Pray today for God to show you something brilliant and beautiful about Him. Sing the song of Psalm 119:

> Be generous with me and I'll live a full life;
>   not for a minute will I take my eyes off your
>   road.
> Open my eyes so I can see
>   what you show me of your miracle-wonders.
> I'm a stranger in these parts;
>   give me clear directions.
> My soul is starved and hungry, ravenous!—
>   insatiable for your nourishing commands.
>   (verses 17–20, MSG)

God works wonders through His Word! Scripture will solve questions in your heart you didn't even know needed to be answered. It will stitch places in your soul you didn't believe could ever be sewn together. It will strengthen your spirit so that you're equipped for the dark world we live in.

When you open your Bible, ask God to open your eyes as well and receive His truth and wisdom.

PRAY

Dear gracious God, thank You for speaking to me through Your Holy Word. Thank You that it is a living and breathing conversation You have with Your children. Help me crave Your Word every day and open my eyes to receive Your revelations. In Jesus's name, amen.

59

SUBMIT IT

The Sovereign LORD is my strength;
he makes my feet like the feet of a deer,
he enables me to tread on the heights.

—HABAKKUK 3:19, NIV

There are days—never-ending days—when we simply feel *done.* I feel them just like you. We all are human and broken and can sometimes feel beaten down.

That's why we can't do this life alone. We can't try running and fighting in our own strength. We need to rely on our heavenly Father, who is "our refuge and strength, an ever-present help in trouble" (Psalm 46:1, NIV).

Life feels hard because it is. We don't just face daily battles; we are in a full-fledged war between faith and fear! This is why we *have* to stay at the feet of Jesus. Buried in His Word. Praying before His holiness. Worshipping Him constantly. Settled in His peace.

But those certain days . . . they certainly come.

Days when everything feels like too much. Days when the Enemy comes and tests our weak spots. And for me, one of those is the struggle of feeling rejected. Some days we feel isolated and alone, and we start to hear those evil whispers.

We have to run to Jesus and believe Him when He says:

> I will be your God throughout your lifetime—
>   until your hair is white with age.
> I made you, and I will care for you.
>   I will carry you along and save you. (Isaiah 46:4)

We have to let Him carry us.

When we try to do it all ourselves, we see how things can go wrong. We see what won't work, what we can't do, that we don't have the knowledge or the education to pull it off. We need to submit all our failures and flaws at His feet.

This is where you will find His strength.

> I can do everything through Christ, who gives me strength. (Philippians 4:13)

Through Christ, we trust what we don't see—that nothing is impossible with God. God is the one who sustains us.

Today, maybe you need to slow down and settle your soul before the Lord. Maybe you need to submit your spirit to His Holy Spirit. Maybe you need to find a sanctuary in the Scriptures.

Dreadful days are going to come. Submit them to God. Find hope in Him who carries you. God is inviting you to come to Him so He can tell you, "We got this!"

PRAY

Dear heavenly Father, thank You for knowing me, for loving me, for protecting me, and for working great things in me. I submit these things that feel too heavy to carry. Please carry them for me. I praise Your name and give You all the glory. In Jesus's name, amen.

60

FOLLOW IT

A third time he asked him, "Simon son of John, do you love me?"

Peter was hurt that Jesus asked the question a third time. He said, "Lord, you know everything. You know that I love you."

Jesus said, "Then feed my sheep."

—JOHN 21:17

"Follow me," Jesus had told Peter and Andrew as He walked the shore of the Sea of Galilee.[1] Years later, those words must have felt distant.

Peter and the disciples had traveled with Jesus, watching Him perform miracles and preach and prophesy many things that were to come. They hadn't fully understood what He said about His coming death. But then on the darkest night, Jesus was taken and crucified. All the disciples could do was run away and hide.

Peter, the bold and brash disciple who once promised Jesus he would follow Him to his death, had done the opposite on that night. He denied Jesus three times. Three very public times. Imagine the remorse that filled him after he learned that Jesus had died.

But the story wasn't over. Jesus had risen from the dead, just as He said He would. He had appeared to the disciples and filled their fearful spirits with joy. "Peace be with you," Jesus had told them.[2]

Did Peter finally get his act together and become the man he was meant to be? No! Even seeing his risen Savior wasn't enough to propel Peter into fulfilling his mission. At the start of John 21, we see that Peter—the impatient, self-doubting Peter—had gone back to fishing. Maybe he didn't understand what Jesus meant when He said to be "fishers of men" (Matthew 4:19, NKJV). Maybe he didn't have the confidence in himself to do it. Maybe the guilt and inadequacy he felt were too much.

When Jesus appeared on the shore of the Sea of Galilee and surprised the disciples by bringing in fish for them to catch, He reminded them of the first time He met them. Jesus undid Peter's denial by asking Peter three times, "Do you love me?" And three times, Peter said yes.

Then Jesus uttered two important words again: "Follow me."

After so many mistakes and mess-ups and mishaps, Peter still got the same chance Jesus gave him years earlier as shown in John 21. "Follow me," Jesus told Peter (verse 19).

Peter had great work to do for Him.

Jesus never gave up on Peter. And He never gives up on us.

Have you heard these words from Jesus? Have you decided to follow Him? Like Peter, we need extra nudges sometimes to kick us out of our old rhythms and into the life God has called us to.

Do you love Jesus? Then follow Him.

Follow Him to the ends of the earth.

Follow Him to fulfill your purpose.

Follow Him to finish your story.

PRAY

Dear gracious God, thank You that no matter how many times I fall down, make mistakes, and lose my way, You never give up on me. You are always asking me to follow You. Help me keep following You today. In Jesus's name, amen.

NOTES

2: Pursue It

1. "I Will Follow," track 13 on Tasha Cobbs Leonard, *Heart. Passion. Pursuit. (Deluxe)*, Motown Gospel, 2017.

3: Read It

1. Alethea L. Blackler et al., "Life Is Too Short to RTFM: How Users Relate to Documentation and Excess Features in Consumer Products," *Interacting with Computers* 28, no. 1 (January 2016): 27–46, https://doi.org/10.1093/iwc/iwu023.

5: Accept It

1. 2 Samuel 5:4.

7: Carry It

1. "One Place," track 6 on Tasha Cobbs Leonard, *One Place Live*, Motown Gospel, 2015.

8: Use It

1. Tasha Cobbs Leonard, "Don't Stop Dreamin!," TikTok video, www.tiktok.com/@tashacobbsleonard/video/69737 01562627656966.

12: Believe It

1. "Gotta Believe," track 16 on Tasha Cobbs Leonard, *10 Years of Tasha*, TeeLee Records, 2023.

15: Do It

1. Maya Moore Irons and Jonathan Irons, *Love and Justice: A Story of Triumph on Two Different Courts* (New York: Andscape Books, 2023).

2. Irons and Irons, *Love and Justice*, 132.

19: Receive It

1. "Grace," track 5 on Tasha Cobbs, *Grace (Live)*, Motown Gospel, 2013.

24: Recognize It

1. 1 Samuel 26:9.

27: Pray It

1. T. D. Jakes, *When Women Pray: 10 Women of the Bible Who Changed the World Through Prayer* (New York: FaithWords, 2020), 13.

2. Joseph Medlicott Scriven, "What a Friend We Have in Jesus," 1855.

29: Release It

1. "Burdens Down," track 3 on Tasha Cobbs Leonard, *Hymns (Live)*, TeeLee Records, 2022.

31: Sing It

1. Fanny Crosby, *Fanny Crosby's Story of Ninety-Four Years* (Grand Rapids, Mich.: Fleming H. Revell Company, 2015), 26.

2. Fanny Crosby, *Fanny J. Crosby: An Autobiography* (Peabody, Mass.: Hendrickson Publishers, 2015), 24.

3. "Fanny Crosby: Prolific and Blind Hymn Writer," *Christianity Today*, accessed March 1, 2024, www.christianitytoday.com/history/people/poets/fanny-crosby.html.

4. "Redeemed, How I Love to Proclaim It!," Fanny Crosby, hymnary.org, https://hymnary.org/text/redeemed_how_i_love_to_proclaim_it.

33: Share It

1. Brené Brown, *Dare to Lead: Brave Work. Tough Conversations. Whole Hearts.* (New York: Random House, 2018), 160.

34: Embrace It

1. Jennifer Justus, "Where the Soul of Nashville Never Dies," The Bitter Southerner, accessed March 2, 2024, https://bittersoutherner.com/soul-of-nashville-the-ryman.
2. "Captain Tom Ryman: Captain. Skeptic. Convert.," Ryman.com, November 2, 2022, www.ryman.com/story/captain-tom-ryman-captain-skeptic-convert.

38: Proclaim It

1. 2 Corinthians 12:9, NIV.

43: Celebrate It

1. Karen Schrock, "Fact or Fiction? An Opera Singer's Piercing Voice Can Shatter Glass," *Scientific American*, August 23, 2007, www.scientificamerican.com/article/fact-or-fiction-opera-singer-can-shatter-glass.

46: Accomplish It

1. "You're Gonna Get the Glory," track 1 on Tasha Cobbs Leonard, *Royalty: Live at the Ryman*, TeeLee Records, 2020.

47: Overcome It

1. "You're Gonna Get the Glory," track 1 on Tasha Cobbs Leonard, *Royalty: Live at the Ryman*, TeeLee Records, 2020.

NOTES

48: Silence It

1. "Joseph and Nicodemus Bury Jesus' Body (19:38–42)," IVP New Testament Commentary Series, BibleGateway, www.biblegateway.com/resources/ivp-nt/Joseph-Nicodemus-Bury-Jesus-Body.

51: Face It

1. See 1 Samuel 17:26.
2. 2 Corinthians 12:7.

52: Encourage It

1. Maya Angelou, *Letter to My Daughter* (New York: Random House, 2008), xii.

53: Remember It

1. John 19:30.

54: Hold It

1. Luke 23:39–41, MSG.
2. Luke 23:42, MSG.
3. Luke 23:43, MSG.
4. "Jesus Saves," track 5 on Tasha Cobbs Leonard, *One Place Live,* Motown Gospel, 2015.

58: Crave It

1. "Now Behold the Lamb," track 2 on Kirk Franklin and the Family, *Christmas,* GospoCentric, 1995.

60: Follow It

1. Matthew 4:19.
2. John 20:26.

ABOUT THE AUTHOR

Two-time Grammy Award—winning singer and songwriter TASHA COBBS LEONARD is one of the most iconic artists in gospel music history. Winner of fifteen GMA Dove Awards, sixteen Stellar Awards, three *Billboard* Music Awards, and two RIAA Certified platinum singles, Tasha was named *Billboard*'s Gospel Artist of the Decade. Alongside her husband, Kenneth Leonard, Jr., she serves as the executive pastor at their church plant, the Purpose Place, in Spartanburg, South Carolina. A successful entrepreneur and owner of several businesses, she launched her own record label, TeeLee Records. Tasha lives in Greenville, South Carolina, with her husband and their four children.

ABOUT THE TYPE

This book was set in Fournier, a typeface named for Pierre-Simon Fournier (1712–68), the youngest son of a French printing family. He started out engraving woodblocks and large capitals, then moved on to fonts of type. In 1736 he began his own foundry and made several important contributions in the field of type design; he is said to have cut 147 alphabets of his own creation. Fournier is probably best remembered as the designer of St. Augustine Ordinaire, a face that served as the model for the Monotype Corporation's Fournier, which was released in 1925.

Believe Bigger. Live Bolder.

In this powerfully inspiring book, Grammy Award-winner Tasha Cobbs Leonard shows us how to stop disqualifying ourselves from what God has called us to do. With conviction borne from her own transformation, Tasha challenges us to a bolder way of life—because taking one more step in faith is always worth it.

Penguin
Random
House